T0108631

Designs on Democracy:

Architecture and Design
in Scotland Post-Devolution

Designs on Democracy:

Architecture and Design
in Scotland Post-Devolution

Stuart MacDonald

Winchester, UK
Washington, USA

First published by Zero Books, 2012
Zero Books is an imprint of John Hunt Publishing Ltd., Laurel House, Station Approach,
Alresford, Hants, SO24 9JH, UK
office1@jhpbooks.net
www.johnhuntpublishing.com
www.zero-books.net

For distributor details and how to order please visit the 'Ordering' section on our website.

Text copyright: Stuart MacDonald 2012

ISBN: 978 1 78099 638 7

All rights reserved. Except for brief quotations in critical articles or reviews, no part of this
book may be reproduced in any manner without prior written permission from the publishers.

The rights of Stuart MacDonald as author have been asserted in accordance with the Copyright,
Designs and Patents Act 1988.

A CIP catalogue record for this book is available from the British Library.

Design: Stuart Davies

Printed in the USA by Edwards Brothers Malloy

We operate a distinctive and ethical publishing philosophy in all
areas of our business, from our global network of authors to
production and worldwide distribution.

CONTENTS

List of Abbreviations

CCA	Centre for Contemporary Arts
CCIs	Creative and Cultural Industries
CEO	Cultural Enterprise Office
DCA	Dundee Contemporary Arts
DCMS	Department of Culture Media and Sport
DTI	Department of Trade and Industry
EC	European Commission
EMBT/RMJM	Enric Miralles Benedetta Tagliabue/Robert Matthew Johnston Marshall
GDP	Gross Domestic Product
GIA	Glasgow Institute of Architects
GVA	Gross Value Added
ICA	Institute of Contemporary Arts
IP	Intellectual Property
LSC	Learning Skills Council
NESTA	National Endowment for Science, Technology and the Arts
SAC	Scottish Arts Council
SCIP	Scottish Creative Industries Partnership
SHEFC	Scottish Higher Education Funding Council
SMEs	Small to Medium Enterprises
R&D	Research and Development
RDA	Regional Development Agency
V&A	Victoria and Albert Museum

Foreword

The Clydesdale and North of Scotland Bank issued a design for its one pound note in 1961 showing an illustration of shipbuilding on the Clyde. The decision to include shipbuilding on a banknote was presumably inspired by the booming self-confidence of the industry as a symbol of economic wealth and stability at the time. 38 years later, in 1999, the Clydesdale Bank issued a £20 note to mark Glasgow's year of celebrations as UK City of Architecture and Design, which featured an illustration of the Lighthouse building, Scotland's National Centre for Architecture and Design, and the dome of Alexander Greek Thomson's Holmwood House on the reverse.

Just as shipbuilding had become part of everyday life in the 1960s and a symbol of our cultural wealth, were we now witnessing the replacement of industry by a new found cultural 'beacon' celebrating the rise of Architecture and Design in the consciousness of the public? Had Architecture and Design moved from being an exclusive pursuit for the benefit of cultural tourism to something much more domestic and everyday that everyone could engage with and enjoy?

In 1999 we could not answer this question but, 13 years on, Stuart MacDonald's collection of writings give us a basis for continuing a very important debate. This is a book representing a 13-year dialogue on behalf of Scotland's creative community. It is a dialogue, which became real in 1999 with the opening of The Lighthouse and the unveiling of the plans for a new Scottish Parliament building. MacDonald had led the £13million development and opening of The Lighthouse and what followed was a successful 8-year reign with focused debate, dissemination and participation surrounding the interface between architecture, design and our environment. MacDonald would use the Lighthouse programme to forge relationships between creative disciplines, while enabling architects and designers to widen their engagement with a new public audience.

Rich with ideas and provocation these 32 papers represent a period of time when 'things happened', the dialogue within these papers includes reference to lectures, exhibitions, press articles, policies, teaching, talking, and new educational practices, which together attempt to shape the future of our cultural and creative landscape. These essays often appear as personal diary entries tracing a thought process through a decade of debate surrounding design in the context of an ever-changing political and economic landscape in Scotland. 'Making' was a big part of this new-found optimism and MacDonald manages to tell the story of architects and designers through their buildings, which ranged in scale and drama from the poetic and political manifestations of a new Scottish Parliament to the more modest interventions into our built environment.

These essays tell the story of people, places and practitioners providing a direction to Scottish design, which propels us out of the stereotypes and myths of being 'Scottish' and into the present. They demonstrate an ability to open up new possibilities for personal, local and national expression.

While these papers map out a very specific timeline of events they also weave together a very unique narrative where for a time design, politics and identity appear to coalesce. MacDonald is clearly a major international authority in the field of design, policy and practice; a person who is evidently a multi-faceted presence: he has spent a decade writing, meeting people, critiquing, travelling, investigating, teaching and advocating while setting out a vision for the creative industries. As Scotland embarks on a road over the next few years to debate the shape of the society we see ourselves in, the acts of our cultural 'ambassadors' like MacDonald will play a very important role.

In 2001 MacDonald makes reference to the Scottish Executive's first policy on architecture in Scotland, which set out forty government commitments intended to help 'raise awareness of the value of good building design; to promote recognition of the importance of architecture to the cultural life of Scotland'. MacDonald's writings are a very timely context as we are about to witness the launch of a new 2012 'Policy on Architecture for Scotland'. As a collection of essays this is already an important archive, which records a remarkable period in time. This was a decade, which has changed Scottish society for the better, Scotland's cultural output has grown, and its creative confidence rose. The New Policy on Architecture will have benefited hugely from this decade of 'doing'. MacDonald's writings are evidence of a creative legacy but importantly they continue a dialogue, which searches for ways to take Scotland forward.

The atmosphere of 1999 and the proceeding decade have played a huge part in shaping the confidence of a number of young architects and designers in Scotland. Many of these practices are now established with enviable portfolios and an international reputation. The exodus of our best students to London slowed right down around this time and a new collective pride in the work being produced North of the border began to emerge. The Lighthouse offered support; exposure and opportunities for young designers while a number of touring exhibitions celebrated the wealth of talent we had been harbouring. NORD was one of these companies, launching in 2002 following the completion of the Tramway redevelopment project. We wanted to be part of the new 'design' debate and The Lighthouse offered the perfect platform. Winning Young British Architecture Practice of the Year at the end of 2006 (YAYA) was wider acknowledgement of what was happening up in Scotland and NORD has much to thank the Lighthouse for during those early years when we were attempting to find our own voice.

When I reflect on my own work as an architect I firmly believe that projects never spring from nothing, and they're never finished once and for all: they continue, they begin again, they return, they become layered over each other and in a similar way this collection of essays are an ongoing conversation that will never be finished.

The debate has to continue...

Alan Pert, Director, NORD Architecture

Introduction

Disasters, pandemics, the War on Terror, iPlayers/Pods/Pads/ Phones, American Idol, the rise of social media or the international banking crisis? Whatever your abiding memories of the Noughties, this was also to some extent a Scottish decade. With devolution, emergent self-government and (for much of the Noughties) a booming economy, a shift took place in Scottish culture with the Scottish Parliament opening in July 1999. However, whether attributable to devolution itself or unforeseen global events, there was something different about this decade. The early Noughties were characterised by anxiety – cynicism even – and in Scotland the escalating costs of the new Parliament building, which opened in 2004, didn't help. At first, Enrique Miralles' design with its poetic interweaving of internationalism and aspiration seemed un-Scottish even though the architect had attempted to create not a building but a landscape into which he could embody the complexity and romanticism of Scottish identity. Its overflow of imagery, iconography, symbolism and metaphor needed time to be absorbed. It's a picture of Scotland that was hard to recognise at first, but now we seem to have grown into it. In many ways, perhaps to the amazement of its critics, the building's seemingly crazy, idiosyncratic, beautiful forms have emerged to shape us, and quite literally, given Scotland a place in the world of architecture. For a time, design, politics and identity appeared to coalesce.

As a controversial manifestation of Noughties' design, the prize-winning Scottish Parliament was at the extreme end of the emblematic scale. But this was also the era of Creative and Cultural Industries, of radical swings in cultural policy and the influence of design on new fields. Design thinking appeared in the curricula of business schools and design became a strategic problem-solving tool and a new discipline – service design –

emerged. Not unconnected with this was the growth of 'prosumption' and changing economic behaviours, and the widespread rise of user-participation and co-creativity and co-design. As well, a growing worldwide interest in applying design methods and design thinking to social and public policy challenges attracted the attention of politicians. So, as well as highlighting a greater demand generally for people to be more involved in decision-making – for greater democracy – and to be the authors of their own narratives, these innovations also heralded an important move to address the interconnected or systemic issues that face modern society; environment, health, welfare, housing, globalisation. But much of this was under the radar and at best of transient interest to the mainstream media, certainly in Scotland. Nonetheless, things happened. The evidence of design-led initiatives, projects, examples, case-studies and innovations suggests a different Scotland to one characterised by cynicism or apprehension.

At the same time as unveiling the Scottish Parliament the Queen opened The Lighthouse, Scotland's Centre for Architecture, Design and the City, the flagship project of Glasgow 1999 UK City of Architecture and Design. And, shortly after-wards the Scottish Executive (now Scottish Government) published the first architecture policy in the UK. Thus, the scene was set, giving design in Scotland a platform that it never had before, as well as providing the starting point for this collection of writings. The collective focus of these essays is the role of design in the democratisation of Scots' lives and experiences; how they can take greater control of and transform their environment, education, homes, health or the services and products they use. They are also about the role of Scottish Government policy and the country's Creative and Cultural Industries' strategy and how these abet or hinder human well-being and prosperity. Simultaneously, this decade-long history of architecture and design post-devolution also distils a narrative about the Lighthouse, the establishment of its democratising mission, the evolution of its transformational strategy and the development of its international programme covering the period of my directorship from 1998 to 2006.

Whilst there are studies of architecture in Scotland post-devolution, corresponding writings on design, beyond the lifestyle sections or newspapers and magazines, are largely non-existent. This collection of essays seeks to fill that gap and ranges over the debates concerning architecture, urbanism, design and the Creative and Cultural Industries and the policies, people and places that stimulate and animate them. Not surprisingly, Miralles' Scottish Parliament building permeates these essays, but not to the exclusion of smaller (and much less expensive) projects right across Scotland. As well as showcasing the spectrum of new architecture from schools to housing to cultural buildings to office spaces, contemporary issues relating to public art, regeneration, heritage and conservation, internationalisation, young architects, and place-making are also featured. Alongside these attention is also drawn to how architects and other people think and talk about buildings and the environment and the attendant social, economic and educational debates.

Creative Industries, closely identified with New Labour, developed in the Noughties into a global phenomenon. Because of their ideological origins Creative Industries are not without their sceptics, but they did nonetheless permit a coherent way of looking at those activities, which trade in creative assets and sit at the crossroads of creativity, business and technology. How Scotland can develop a sustainable and competitive economy and how Creative Industries insert themselves into the debate about architecture and design, weaves its way through these essays. Crucial in this sense was the interdisciplinary character of much of the Lighthouse's work and the way in which projects transected architecture, design, urbanism and art. The changing context for this work is also discussed and embraces shifts in contemporary culture and creativity from craft to digital design to the creative class itself.

The thread that interconnects these essays is the issue of participation and the democratisation of design and imaginative ways of making this happen. This weaves its way through the essays from innovations in exhibition making pioneered by the Lighthouse involving co-production and co-creation, to user-centred approaches in design education and public engagement. Importantly, these essays also tell a story about Scotland's creative practitioners – about the people behind the anonymous Government analyses and statistics that are typical of the sector: where they work; the difficulties they encounter; and how their ideas and what they create and design contribute to Scotland's democratic culture and identity.

A Beacon for Scotland

Reaching out and drawing in. The Lighthouse is a timely creation given the current, popular interest in design matters. The opening of the The Lighthouse as Scotland's centre for Architecture, Design and the City is timely, not least because Enric Miralles' vision for the Edinburgh parliament building has captured the public imagination, opening up a debate about architecture, democracy and the nature of cultural identity. At the same time, the community is questioning the relationship between architects and clients, cities and citizenship and how we can negotiate the future. With its mission to educate, to engage, to reach out and to innovate, The Lighthouse is particularly well placed to address the contemporary need to involve the public in issues to do with the built environment and mass-produced objects. The Lighthouse sees architecture and design as social, educational and economic concerns which are important to everyone.

Page and Park's conversion of The Lighthouse building facilitates that aspiration, superbly. The industrial toughness of the building translates well into flexible spaces for arrange of purposes, such as education, exhibitions, conferences, Design into Business, a Charles Rennie Mackintosh interpretation centre, and facilities for cafes and a shop. Also, Page and Park's two new extensions, one, nicknamed the 'battery pack' which has created the entrance, circulation and additional exhibition space, the other called the 'Dow' after the building was demolished to make way for office, store and workshop space, have added considerably to The Lighthouse's muscle in terms of access through the building and smaller galleries.

The Lighthouse's development is a model of partnership with

contributions from the Scottish Arts Council Lottery Fund, the National Heritage Lottery Fund, Historic Scotland, the European Regional Development Fund, The Glasgow Development Agency, Glasgow City Council and, not least, facilitation from the Glasgow 1999 Festival Company. This pulling together of resources towards a mutually agreed objective exemplifies the direction The Lighthouse might take in the future.

Debates about the value of architecture centres focus on the fact that architecture is physical and environmental; it is out there. Architecture cannot necessarily be experienced in the same way as fine art in a gallery. But the Lighthouse in itself offers an architectural experience. The way the Centre is sensed by visitors is a formative one. You enter through contemporary glass and steel, and then ascend the building by escalator moving past traditional materials – sandstone, tiles and brick. The effect of the tactile surfaces making up the back of the Mackintosh building is strong and offers a brilliant contrast to the lightness of the newer materials of the 'battery pack'. This intimate sensation of the building's construction is even more forceful as you climb the original tower – the suspended staircase takes you into close contact with massive and roughly hewn sandstone blocks, particularly as the tower corbels out. You become aware of the creative tension between the old and the new, the sensuousness of the materials, stylistic differences, changes in building technology and the sheer physicality of the architecture.

This induction into the world of architecture through a physical experience is continued when visitors climb up into either the old tower or new viewing platform. Depending on their point of view, visitors can look out over the city Mackintosh and his Victorian and Edwardian peers helped to create. Alternatively, the history of architecture can be enjoyed in rooftop microcosm from David Hamilton's classical Royal Exchange to Wyllie Shanks' Corbusier-like College of Building and Printing. As well as interpretive visitor materials relating to this built experience, The Lighthouse has also created a guide to its urban setting, highlighting the uniqueness of Glasgow's grid plan, and celebrating architectural achievements such as the Art Deco extravagance of Burton's shop and Gillespie, Kidd and Coia's copper-clad infill building at the entrance to Mitchell Lane.

The Lighthouse also offers novel virtual experiences – Strathclyde University's ABACUS computer model of the city and Glasgow School of Art's Digital Design Studio that describes Glasgow's industrial design heritage. Public engagement with architecture and design is expanded through the education centre – purpose-designed and one of the largest within any institution of its kind – which, with its range of spaces for children and adults, will allow visitors to play and learn creatively. It is in education and community outreach that The Lighthouse intends to break new ground, working with the public on design problems in the real world, building on the success of Glasgow 1999's education and community initiative programmes. This proactive policy of including people in design and architecture also applies to exhibitions. Apart from offering a wide range of exhibitions, the aim is to make them interactive, complimenting them with workshops, lectures and other activities.

This sets the agenda for a number of interrelated themes – the learning city, the creative city, the connected city. Running through these themes is the recognition that people are the key resources in the sustainability of our cities. The Lighthouse will communicate this agenda outwards whilst respecting local needs, working with its partners both here in Scotland and abroad.

2

The Lighthouse: Architecture and Design Centre or Multiplex?

Introduction

The Lighthouse – Scotland's Centre for Architecture, Design and the City to give it its full title – is quite a new form of cultural institution. It sees architecture and design as social, educational, economic and cultural concerns which affect everyone. Immediately, therefore, in terms of the visitor experience and that multi-functional mission, the Lighthouse has to conquer a whole set of psychological and social barriers because to many people architecture and design are still elite and intimidating.

To start with the building, however. The Lighthouse is a conversion of Charles Rennie Mackintosh's Glasgow Herald building. It is very much about modernity both at the end of the nineteenth and the beginning of the twenty-first centuries. Mackintosh's sinuous Art Nouveau lines deconstructed the classical vocabulary of the time and heralded (literally) its function as a media centre and centre for technology. The twentieth century design conversion draws on the language of Glasgow's contemporary bars and clubs whilst making references to the city's industrial past. That identification with Glasgow and Scotland's industrial heritage and design inventiveness is very important to the Lighthouse. It gives a sense of identity and purpose and acts as a symbol for the city's creativity and its burgeoning creative industries. Opening up that creativity to a whole number of audiences is its principal mission. Designed to be multifunctional, depending on who you are, the Lighthouse is at once visitor attraction, heritage centre, gallery, education centre, café, business centre, conference venue, network hub – multiplex. So how do we draw people in and what do we give them?

Marketing with Mackintosh

Macintosh is a good starting point. Clearly, there is a cultural tourist market for Mackintosh, his work and that of his circle, but there is also a significant local and educational market. We have a Charles Rennie Mackintosh Centre and we use his popularity and accessibility quite unashamedly. If you can develop an interest in Mackintosh then that's the beginning of an understanding of European Modernism and from that you can move on to more contemporary themes. The 'Mack' Centre combines audio-visual interactivity with very physical contact with the building and the city – closeness to actual architecture and perceptions of the city are an important part of the visitor experience. We also multiply this alignment of heritage and modernity with bus tours of Mackintosh buildings and contemporary Glasgow and other cultural tourist type activities. Moving all this along is a Mackintosh Interpretation officer supported by the Heritage Lottery Fund whose role is to work with school and community groups and visitors and provide a springboard to the wider activities of the Lighthouse.

Exhibitions

As Aaron Betsky has asked recently, who needs design museums? His point being that such institutions, despite their avowed aims of drawing non-specialist audiences really attract professionals and students. Architecture and design exhibitions - usually with models or objects on plinths or unfathomable drawings – are notoriously difficult for the lay public to understand. However, exhibitions are an important way of engaging the public and with 300,000 visitors in our first year we can maybe lay some claim to breaking down barriers. It should also be said that we are the only ticketed cultural venue in Glasgow, a city with a long tradition of free entry to its many museums and galleries and that we have introduced entry charges with little difficulty. It should also be said that unwaged, OAPs and children get in free.

Our exhibition policy is to avoid objects on plinths and to try to use successful ideas from the fine art world and also to mount exhibitions which have a high degree of interactivity, digital or video content, or which create novel content by looking at the relationship between art, design and architecture. In that way we believe we can widen and engage our audience. Take two exhibitions, which are on just now at the Lighthouse that we have curated and used Glasgow-based exhibition designers. Firstly, Droog, the first large scale showing in the UK of the Dutch design phenomenon. The Droog foundation has achieved a lot of recognition in terms of the world of professional design; they star every year in Milan and their products are represented in almost every major museum in the world. The idea here was to place Droog designs in Glaswegians' homes, for people to live with them and to create video diaries of people's reactions to the objects. As well as being a new way of curating design, for the visitor the exhibition puts the objects – which for many people are quite strange – in the context of readily identifiable responses and in a register with which they feel comfortable. The accents are Glaswegian not double Dutch.

Connecting Cultures, the second exhibition, was curated and designed by Glasgow design consultancy Graven Images. Through the medium of people working in the creative industries, the idea was for visitors learn about issues of cultural diversity, anti-racism and how Scottish and other ethnic identities, be they Pakistani or Polish, evolve and change. There is a lot of different content in the show presented in quite a novel way, interviews with the designers, artists or architects, mementos and memorabilia in revolving drums and a whole range of different forms of design from landscape art to jewellery. And, visitors (courtesy of Polaroid) can be photographed and archived by the National Museum of Scotland as part of a 'Diversity Charter'; so there is the opportunity of becoming part of the exhibition. Connecting Cultures aims to break down all sorts of barriers – cultural, social – as well exploding the boundaries between architecture, art and design. It goes without saying that through an exhibition like this and its accompanying education and public programme, we hope to attract a new audience and draw in communities who might not normally be interested in architecture or design.

Education

We are also conscious of the need to develop an audience from as early an age as possible and we are fortunate in having one entire floor of the Lighthouse given over to life-long learning. The Wee People's City – a model of Glasgow in miniature – demonstrates a commitment to taking design to a section of the community that is often neglected; that is, families and very young children. It includes interactive buildings including a church whose denomination can be changed by altering the roof design; there are communication networks, projected fly-throughs of the cityscape; building materials to play with and an architectural alphabet to aid creative play. It aims to involve all the senses in an imaginative way to grow audiences from an early age. The education facility has its own dedicated gallery, very good workshop space for groups of all ages and a computer laboratory. Interestingly, our visitor analyses indicted that a high proportion of our local visitors come because their children have been at the Lighthouse through school or through our workshop programme. Word of mouth, even in a city the size of Glasgow is a hugely important marketing tool. But we also have a community outreach team. This is funded by the National Lotteries Charity Board and the team's brief is to work with disadvantaged communities and to develop design projects with them like this example from last year when Glasgow was UK City of Architecture and Design. It is also important to say that like our exhibitions there is a high degree of digital content in projects like this. Using computers to design, whether it is lighting or the design of a play park breaks down barriers.

As an architecture centre we are also very aware of the context of the venue, in other words the urban treasure – 'the invisible city' – that is on our doorstep and how we can encourage people to engage with it. Our inspiration is Italo Calvino but also the model proposed by Rock and Sellars – the Museum of the Ordinary, a project derived from the urban grid or Manhattan but transposed to the network of lanes in Glasgow city centre. The aim, to celebrate the ordinary, attempts to release any institutional blockage or control by inviting the nearby public – business people, shoppers, school kids – to become curators, public artists, critics. The Museum of the Ordinary is now a long-term research project initiated by the Lighthouse in partnership with a number of bodies.

Other Audiences

Interactive exhibitions, education, helping eliminate social exclusion and drawing in diverse communities are very important in developing a wide audience but we also have a business or corporate audience. For example, we house a major economic project, the Glasgow Design Initiative, which has its own professional audience of designers and manufacturers, and we work in partnership with that initiative on conferences, seminars and exhibitions which promote design to the business community. We also have a booming conference business. This brings in another kind of audience, who incidentally, as well as funding many of our activities, are as much attracted by the Lighthouse's cultural activities as they are by our conference facilities. In that way commercial and educational activities can compliment one another with no compromise to our central mission. In a similar kind of way retail is seen as another way of growing an audience. We are of course concerned to promote the work of young designers whether it is El Ultimo Gritto from

London or VK&C from Glasgow. This provides the opportunity to sell work which cannot be bought anywhere else and introduce contemporary cutting edge design to a new public.

Conclusion

Developing the offering to visitors for us, therefore, is about creating a multi-level and multi-layered experience. It is about appreciating that the needs and interests of visitors or users are not uniform. Differentiation is key. Equally, it is important to recognise that members of the public, however you define them, do not perceive architecture and design in the same way as architects and designers. Nor do they see the boundaries between cultural forms in the same way. If a newish cultural institution like the Lighthouse, which is not publicly funded, is to survive, then it must engage with a range of audiences and promote policies about exhibitions and education (including inreach and outreach) by reflecting cultural democracy, getting architecture and design off plinths and into the hands of its clients and taking account of the external environment – real life in other words – which is the ultimate context for architecture and design. Sustainability for us is contingent upon offering a differentiated service to visitors and recognising that the world is as much about social and economic regeneration as it is about education and entertainment, and that these things needn't be separate.

3

An Art Lesson Glasgow has to Learn

Gateshead's Angel of the North, Birmingham's Centenary Square, Cardiff's Art in the Bay – even New York's ubiquitous cows – all testify to the role of public art in creating a sense of place and expressing civic aspiration. Glasgow's Victorian forebears knew what they were doing when they commissioned the statues, memorials and fountains, which enrich the city's streets and parks. This incomparable legacy was a demonstration of commercial strength and gave the city its identity.

A lot has been done to celebrate that heritage. Recently, Ray MacKenzie's 'Sculpture in Glasgow' and the earlier 'Glasgow Revealed' re-awaked people to the treasure above people's heads. The more recent announcement that Glasgow's fountains will flow again, meaning the restoration of the Doulton, Stewart Memorial and three other fountains, is welcome from both a historic and an environmental point of view.

What about contemporary public art? What defines Glasgow as a twenty-first century city? Modernism, which dominated most of last century, is out. Few complained about the removal of the 'blob' bronze from Buchanan Street. Figurative art is fashionable again and the range of materials and media available to today's artists offers countless possibilities. Glasgow also has a glittering array of artists and designers. Can the city re-establish its historic lead? McKenzie's prediction is that it will. Initiatives on the edge of the city centre like the Crown Street Regeneration Project or Glasgow 1999's Millennium Spaces show that diverse, accessible and engaging artistic developments are not only possible but that people actually want them. Likewise the regeneration of Glasgow's public realm will have a major impact on the city centre but whilst there is little debate about quality or the attention to detail, questions keep surfacing about the role of public art in that context.

The crowds thronging George Square in July to see the International Sand Sculpture Festival showed a popular appetite for art. Simultaneously, the City supported Stephen Skrynka's much more conceptual Tunnel. Apart from revealing a trend for temporary events in the public domain, projects like this might give a pointer. Short-term happenings can engage a wide audience without making the city a permanent hostage to artistic fortune.

Today's urban community has diverse needs and interests. The idea of public art is new and is changing, as is the concept of private and public space. The Victorians who endowed Glasgow's built heritage meant the public to be edified and educated. Present day citizens want to be entertained. They use the public realm more for private than public reasons. This poses enormous problems for those who believe that contemporary art can be potent way of expressing a city's aspiration and identity.

Great strides have been made within the city centre in creating a viable public art arising from a dialogue with people, artists, architects and those responsible for urban regeneration. That ambitious lesson could be applied to the centre and the renewed public realm. With the Lighthouse the city now has the ideal platform for that debate.

4

Why Do We Need Art Schools?

Why Architecture/Design Centres? Why Art Schools?

What I thought it would be useful to talk about, since I run the Lighthouse, Scotland's National Architecture and Design Centre, and you are from the school of art, is why we need architecture and design centres and, indeed, why we need schools of art? Especially in the light of the funding council's recent reallocation, which does the art schools no favours, despite the importance of the creative/cultural industries to Scotland's economy.

On the way I am going to touch on what I think are relevant contemporary themes – like the creative and cultural industries, creative cities – and take a look at what these things mean in today's Scotland. And, I might also take a sideswipe at modern art.

In Praise of Mongrels

If indeed there is any point at all in what I am going to talk about it is in praise of what Philip Dodds, director of the ICA in London, calls mongrels; mongrel institutions like the Lighthouse and like art schools but which, because we are mongrels, are difficult to pigeon-hole – particularly for funding bodies like SHEFC or SAC.

The End of Art

My starting point is Arthur Danto's famous essay about art 'After the End of Art' and what it means when art can be anything? I think this is quite important because for Fine Art it has signaled a move to ideas over say, aesthetics. It is also to have meant a widening of the definition of art to include, for example, architecture and design as well as all the things that are now organised under the creative industries cluster. Design and architecture are also, of course, about ideas. They are also about a lot of other things such as commerce – they are commodified – but then so is fine art. The winner of this year's Turner prize, who is a commercial photographer, is a good example. But like art, design can now also be anything. If you look at the Design Council's Millennium Products initiative, the definition ranges from a drug to aid sexual performance, Viagra, to a piece of business software. So we have a post-modern soup that affects equally art, architecture and design; it affects you as educators as much as it affects me as architecture/design centre director. And, it is a soup in which cultural, economic, social and educational issues are also swimming.

No-brainer

There is an over-riding issue here. There is a temptation for some people to rail on about the commodification of culture. It's not about that. Nor for that matter is it about dumbing down as against braining up. The debate is about engaging with culture at whatever level imaginatively and creatively. But there are at least three problems with that thesis. Firstly, culture is still treated narrowly and we don't have a widened definition of art. You can see this everywhere. It is evident in the art school curriculum, which remains based on the nineteenth century model. Maybe that model is still robust; I don't know? You can also see it in SAC's continued bailing out of Scottish Opera. If you count up how many millions have been spent on opera since the end of Second World War and think what the visual arts could have achieved with that investment it really doesn't bear thinking about. Secondly, we live in a society which pays lip service to the value of creativity and imagination despite all the Government's exhortations about creativity and the creative industries. Thirdly, we need new ways of talking about creativity and culture. We need a new narrative.

The Allure of Modern Art

However, to come back to modern art. I think this is important for all of us and to what I am trying to develop here. Modern art has a tremendous allure. We have the undoubted regeneration successes of Tate Modern, Walsall and of course DCA. I think the numbers going to those places are fantastic and long may it continue. Whether or not I am convinced those visitors actually understand what they see (and I am not) I don't think really matters. What I do think matters is the fact that there is now an acceptance of modern art, largely because modern art has been commodified. The Guggenheim is now a brand and it has its own brand architecture. Hugh Pearman, the architecture critic of the *Sunday Times*, has said that people go to galleries not to engage with the collection or the building but for the modern art experience – the Bilbao or the Tate Modern experience. Sheltered accommodation for the avant-garde as cultural critic Robert Hewison puts it. Artists like Tracy Emin and Damien Hirst have been complicit in this. Think of the value of their intellectual capital and how they trade with it. I also think in that same context a lot of the territory which once belonged to fine art, like the visual dimension and the visual aesthetic, is now the domain of ad agencies and image makers. So, where does that take us?

The Exclusion of Design and Architecture

You must to understand that I am not being negative nor am I uncritical. I think if you are an educator – or for that matter someone who runs an architecture and design centre – this is hugely interesting; it offers a vast amount of material, a vast amount of knowledge, to be interrogated and harvested. It underlines what I said about the importance of engaging with culture at any level creatively and imaginatively. The issue is really about whether by ascribing a commercial value to something you are in danger of excluding someone. Access is, therefore, key. But the point I am coming to is why the preoccupation with Fine Art – installation and conceptual art along with painting – over design and architecture. Compare the current status of design and architecture with art – is it the same? What's different? What you don't see at Tate Modern, unlike MOMA or the Pompidou, is contemporary architecture and design cheek by jowl with art. Yet Britain is a world leader in design, especially fashion. Are we in some form of denial? Are we, because of some form of reverse psychology, in danger of excluding architecture and design, culturally and socially? I'll come back to that.

Why Do We Need Design Museums?
To many people design and architecture are still alien, intimidating or elite. What design is really about are not superficialities of taste or style as many cultural critics would like to pigeon hole it, instead it's about our efforts to define and control the human environment. Contemporary design and architecture can also be a powerful conveyor of ideas. So, there are powerful environmental, social and economic, as well as cultural reasons, for engaging with design.

The Lighthouse
The Lighthouse is not, therefore, essentially concerned with issues of design curatorship, theory, or history but more with getting architecture and design into people's life-streams. That's why we treat it socially, culturally and economically. That is also, I think, where we have common cause with schools of art because of the high premium you place on practicality. If it has taken this long to get to the Lighthouse I'll now try and explain some of the ways that we are trying to do that and how we are working with schools of art and, hopefully, in the process point up the importance of both the Lighthouse and institutions like Duncan of Jordanstone.

Creative Industries and Education

The reason we are here today, planning a series of follow up workshops and other activities to a big national conference at Dundee Contemporary Arts (DCA) on the creative industries and education — is a really good example. The importance of the creative industries to the national economy, their relationship to education and how we can create better support systems to develop, nurture and sustain new talent ought to be a major priority. So this partnership with The Lighthouse, Duncan of Jordanstone, Scottish Enterprise, NESTA and the Design Council has filled a significant gap. It is also another example of 'mongrelness'. People look at the creative industries and tend to pick out the bits they are interested in. These are usually discipline specific like software development or architecture. Alternatively, they are cynical. They miss out the fact that what is really happening in cities like Glasgow and Dundee is that it is not just platforms that are converging, it is disciplines as well. Look at a games software company like Red Lemon that contains an extraordinary range of disciplines. For art schools (it seems to me) the trick is to be aware of what is happening and to get that awareness across. It should permeate and infect the art school at all levels. It is not necessarily about creating all sorts of new courses.

Creative Cities

There is also a point to be made about cities. Both Glasgow and Dundee are post-industrial cities. As the rubric in that context goes, whereas jute, steel, coal, jam were once the prime industrial resources, in a post-industrial sense, people and their creativity are now the key resources. If the question is, how can citizens be helped to gain a stake in their own futures, then the parallel question is what is the role of art schools and what about cultural institutions? Are current formats appropriate to this new narrative? How can cities support the creative economy? And, this brings me back to why we need more than ever, mongrel institutions that can respond to the changing environment. And I mean respond quickly.

Mongrel Partnerships

Maybe what I mean is we need more mongrel partnerships. If you think of the phenomenal cultural regeneration of Glasgow and now Dundee – places that a few years ago people would have laughed their heads off at in the context of culture – what is interesting is to think how acceptance of that cultural regeneration has come about. One of the reasons is certainly new partnerships. DCA, the university and the City is a case in point. One of the things the Lighthouse is currently interested in is creative networks and how you can generate new ideas. Networks and creativity are intrinsically symbiotic. To maximise benefits, networking needs to become even more intense and with new configurations. We have just been awarded a grant from NESTA to do just that.

The Architecture of Networks

The architecture of networks is the new thing. I am not going to go on about this too much. But what is the motivation for networking in the context of culture or creativity? The answer is we need to plot the future – we need an urban vision. Scotland's city economies are crucial to its future success. But cities as political entities won't network. Their trigger is usually crisis. But the Lighthouse and Duncan of Jordanstone can and we can draw in other parties. More importantly we can operate beyond the banalities of best practice or best value. The fact that Scottish Enterprise is supportive of what we are doing or that the Scottish Executive are funding the Scottish Council Foundation which is also a partner networker, shows there is a need for new narratives, new networks and new ways of thinking about cities.

Conclusion

So, I know have talked at a pretty abstract level and put the focus of the art school and the Lighthouse on cities. I know that there are many other things we could focus on. Like global capitalism and trading IP rights, which will have a huge impact on design in the Third World particularly, and which is well described by Naomi Klein in her book *No Logo*. But you cannot separate your future from that of the city of Dundee any more than we can separate ours from Glasgow. Together, though, we can create a totally new dialogue about Scotland, one that is based on creativity and imagination. What we really need is a bill of cultural rights. The old partnerships, the old networks, the old ways of talking are not going to deliver that.

5

Progressive Pragmatism

Art for Regeneration's Sake

The 5th of November 2000, when Cardiff's Centre for Visual Arts shut its doors for the last time, was a sad day. As more and more cities compete for everything – resources, tourists, and inward investment – the prospect of any capital city without a high-class venue for the visual arts would seem to be artistically and economically suicidal. As a regular visitor to Cardiff, I can testify to the dearth of anything culturally worthwhile to visit, certainly as far as the late twentieth and twenty-first centuries go. The Centre for Visual Arts was a glimmer on a pretty gloomy horizon. As Jonathan Jones has pointed out, the Centre for Visual Arts was doomed from the start, not least because it started life with a funding shortfall and there was no way its public body stakeholders were ever likely to plug the gap. A self-fulfilling prophecy almost, and a salutary lesson in the history of Lottery arts funding. At more or less the same time as the Centre for Visual Arts came into being, 400 miles away, Glasgow launched The Lighthouse, a £12.5 million conversion of Charles Rennie Mackintosh's Glasgow Herald building. There are many similarities: historic city centre restoration, culture as urban renewal, attendant issues of culture as consumption and, of course, large inputs of Lottery cash. That said, there are more differences than similarities; they are to do with history, context and having a pragmatic vision (having a flexible building helps as well). The Lighthouse is now getting into its stride, robustly looking to the future. The Cardiff Centre's demise and The Lighthouse's relative success make for an illuminating case study.

The Need for a Creative History

The major distinction between the two projects is that The Lighthouse is in Glasgow. The city resurrected itself from a post-industrial black hole through cultural regeneration by using a number of strategies, notably a series of high profile festivals – the Garden Festival, European City of Culture, Year of Visual Arts – and, most recently, UK City of Architecture and Design. According to a DEMOS report, the city is the focus of a burgeoning creative industries sector. In short, Glasgow is buzzing. Its galleries, bars, cafes and regenerated city centre buildings form a backdrop to a highly creative culture. Importantly, although the use of the arts in urban renewal is new, Glasgow as a vibrant cultural centre is not. Its imposing Victorian architecture, including the inestimable Charles Rennie Mackintosh heritage and the collections of the Glasgow School in its galleries, testify to the creativity of the late nineteenth and early twentieth centuries. This legacy is enormously important in making the city a cultural entity. Nor can you forget that Glasgow was the second city of the Empire and an industrial design centre second to none in the world.

Visitor Attraction or Multiplex?

The Glasgow backdrop is important to understanding the position of The Lighthouse. It is not simply a visitor centre; it is a multiplex, which gives all sorts of people access to two major forms of contemporary culture, architecture and design. It provides a novel venue for conferences and events, acts as an umbrella for a range of lifelong learning activities, and promotes the creative industries. All of this is done in tandem with an array of partners. The problem with the Centre for Visual Arts was that it focused too much on being a visitor attraction and was over-dependent on door income from visitors. However, key to comprehending why The Lighthouse is flourishing is to ask – and maybe Cardiff should have asked a similar question – why do

Glasgow and Scotland need an architecture and design centre?

The Lighthouse as UK Design Centre

In London right now a debate is raging about the conversion of yet another power station, Battersea, by Nicholas Grimshaw, and how it might become not only London's, but also the UK's design centre. Despite a variety of views, there is consensus that the last thing London needs is another visitor attraction. What is needed, pundits reckon, is a mongrel organisation that supports the creative industries, promotes the best of UK design and nurtures young talent. Some months ago *Blueprint* – one of the world's leading design magazines – stated that London could no longer claim to be the UK's design centre because of the existence of centres such as The Lighthouse. In many ways, The Lighthouse is already doing what is proposed for Battersea.

Securing International Credibility

How can that claim be justified? Firstly, The Lighthouse in its short existence has proved to be one of the most visited architecture and design centres anywhere, despite the fact that it is not solely a visitor attraction. London's Design Museum gets only 150,000 annual visitors and the lavishly funded Netherlands Architecture Institute in Rotterdam even fewer. The Lighthouse does better than either and, importantly, draws its audience from a wider base. Secondly, Glasgow's centre has equally rapidly developed an international reputation, and The Lighthouse and its programmes have been the subject of conferences from Paris to New York. Partnerships have been created with a whole range of like-minded centres around the world. The reason this has happened is that The Lighthouse has broad appeal, which is the result of very proactive education and outreach strategies allied to a diverse exhibition and events programme. Much of this has been cutting-edge, like the development of a virtual architecture centre, which will break down all sorts of barriers; the Design Olympics, in which every kid is a winner; and the Museum of the Ordinary, which is about involving all sorts of people in thinking about contemporary architecture and design and what it means to them. Strategic partnerships lead to innovation.

Achieving a number of UK 'firsts' is another factor. Like mounting the first exhibition of amazing Dutch architectural practice MVRDV; hosting the first major show of the 'Droog' design phenomenon; defying convention with 'Connecting Cultures', an exhibition celebrating cultural diversity as well as demonstrating the range of today's design, which confounded its cynics by getting 40,000 visitors and drawing in a new audience; and linking Scotland's new strategy on the creative industries with creativity in the world of education. None of these events was predicated on large revenue income or income derived from ticket sales. The funds came from an astute range of partnerships. Additionally, about 50% of the posts in The Lighthouse are funded by external bodies.

Progressive Pragmatism

Probably the greatest divergence is that The Lighthouse, whilst always keeping sight of its cultural and educational mission, believes – as does Scotland's new first minister, Henry McLeish – in 'progressive pragmatism'. In other words, recognising change in the external environment and being responsive to it. So, expanding the conference business is seen as being as much a part of audience development as is doing educational outreach in a peripheral housing scheme. Design retail is viewed as a crucial element in exhibition interpretation. The built heritage is seen as vital in drawing an audience that can then be converted to contemporary architecture and design. Lifelong learning is rooted in local and national strategy. Running through all of this are two parallel golden threads. Firstly, a respect for the Glaswegian audience, recognising that Glasgow is neither Milan nor London. Secondly, a conscious desire to ground Lighthouse policy in national policy. Co-terminous with devolution, Scotland is unique in having interconnected policies for Culture, Architecture and the Creative Industries, and The Lighthouse sees itself as instrumental to the delivery of those policies. If you dedicate yourself purely to being 'a visitor attraction' you imperil the future. A mixed economy is the sensible approach. Not only that, if you are in an environment in which reinvention is paramount to long-term survival – and this has been central to Glasgow's post-industrial renaissance 'progressive pragmatism' have to be the watchwords.

6

Subverting Design

Introduction

This paper proceeds on the basis that contemporary design, and architecture exhibitions particularly, are inherently problematic. This is not helped by the fact that there isn't really any literature on such exhibitions and their curation (unless I am missing something). Therefore, the focus of this paper is The Lighthouse, Scotland's Centre for Architecture and Design, and its experience in the two years it has been in existence, of subverting design and architecture through its exhibition programme to overtake its mission of bringing those two cultural forms – design and architecture, that is, to a wide audience.

Who needs design or architecture exhibitions?

Design museums, despite their claims about wanting to develop a broad audience, tend in the main to attract professionals and students. Comparative study of design or architecture museums and how they approach exhibition curation throws up interesting issues. Basically, they do not attract the same numbers as fine art venues. For example, London's Design Museum attracts only 150,000 visitors a year. And, whether it is the Canadian Centre for Architecture, Arc En Reve architecture centre in Bordeaux, Sweden's Arkitectur Museet or the Netherlands Architecture Institute, the visitor numbers are similarly low.

It is interesting in this context that the world's most visited architecture centre, sadly now pulled down, was Berlin's Info Box on Potzdamer Platz. With thousands of people queuing to get in daily, the stars in this instance were the actual buildings. Although it did not style itself as an architecture centre, it most surely was one. The lesson here is that while architecture is popular, architecture in museums is not. This would seem to be confirmed by Victoria Thornton director of Architecture Dialogue who has said that architecture exhibitions are seen by the profession as an intellectual exercise, and anything other than that is seen as populist. She sees this as one of the dilemmas holding the issue back, asking what other art form substitutes direct experience for a photograph on the wall?

The Lighthouse, I will argue, would appear to have broken through such barriers. With over half a million visitors since opening two years ago we seem to be creating a genuinely democratic and accessible centre. It may be salient to attempt to explain how and why by taking some examples of exhibitions and their curation from that brief history.

Critical Context

Objects on plinths be they chairs or other artifacts, architectural models – and even more difficult architectural drawings – are notoriously difficult for the lay public to understand. Claire Catterall, one the most interesting of the new breed of design curators – 'Stealing Beauty' (ICA, London spring 1999) and 'Food' (Glasgow, summer 1999) – believes that no-one is doing good design exhibitions: 'the Design Museum does boring one-liners on modern masters'. Sue Andrew, like Catterall, another former Design Museum curator, attempted with 'Winning: The Design of Sport' (Glasgow,1999) to attract new audiences. In Andrews' words, 'at the end of the creative process Winning was, in fact, an old fashioned exhibition, in that it simply encouraged visitors to look'.

Despite the popularity of the subject and the accessibility of contemporary sport objects in shops the exhibition failed to deliver the immediacy and tactility of the high street. Vertigo – the strange new world of the contemporary city, another Glasgow 1999 exhibition, curated by Rowan Moore and designed by architects Caruso St John, was criticised for being too po-faced and lacking the vibrancy and fascination of the present-day subjects of the exhibitions.

Example

In the Lighthouse our exhibition policy is to avoid objects on plinths and to try to use successful ideas from, retail, television, even the fine art world – anywhere really – to mount exhibitions which have a high degree of interactivity, digital or video content, and which create novel content by looking at the relationship between art, design, architecture and the creative industries. In that way we believe we can widen and engage our audience. Even in the case of exhibitions, which have been shown primarily for commercial reasons – and these have tended to be young design or new media companies or important local initiatives – we have attempted to make them at least visually accessible and engaging. 'Electric City' was an example of an exhibition in this context. It presented to the public a representative archive of the last three decades of contemporary urban music in Glasgow and its interconnection with design. It aimed to show how strongly music has been part of the life of the city and how Glasgow has been, at different times, an essential centre in the national scene, as well as a place with a healthy and diverse musical underground. Curated by Modern Institute, the exhibition included a specially devised bar area and dance floor comprising the club interior from the legendary Berlin Club WMF and a psychedelic floor by Jim Lambie.

Shown in the form of an archive, the show displayed visual material, a collection of recordings, archive video and a comprehensive series of contemporary interviews with important figures. This archive cum exhibition aimed to be entertaining but also to provide real information, and plenty of material, which had never been seen in public before. Over 120 bands, venues and individuals were represented by music, photos, interviews, articles, artworks, fanzines, and memorabilia of all kinds.

Compilation CDs put together by DJs and musicians charted influences on Glasgow music. Design and photography was highlighted in the posters and pictures, which covered the walls of the exhibition space. Electric City tried to create an environment which reflected the nature of the show's subject, drawing on clubs and music venues for its design approach, with plenty of seats, listening posts and a cafe, encouraging visitors to stay and spend time enjoying the wealth of material in the show. It also became, temporarily, an integral part of the contemporary Glasgow scene, presenting the best new bands and club/lounge nights in the city, and providing a platform for events. Importantly, it drew in a new audience.

Architectural Didactics

This subversive educational aspect has been referred to by Bart Lootsma, the Dutch architectural curator and critic, in one of the few books devoted to architecture exhibitions. He talks about this in the context of discerning three broad tendencies: the first is architecture exhibitions as prime media events; the second is renewed attention on the city as a product of larger social processes; and thirdly, a concern for education, not necessarily through an overt role, but by broadening the reach of the museum. The two latter trends are certainly where we are. Lootsma has also said that a didactic concept is paramount when presenting architecture, even more so than when presenting art.

Digital Real

I want to conclude by reiterating the need to involve what it seems to me is the prime resources of architecture and design exhibitions – people and the environment they live in. A Lighthouse exhibition that has just finished is Digital Real. Digital Real is, however, more than an exhibition. It is a revolutionary education programme focussed in on the Creative Industries. It is located in Glasgow's peripheral estates working with young people who, typically, have rejected or have been rejected by the system. Also, it has involved graduates of Duncan of Jordanstone. Five areas within the Creative Industries have been identified: urban design, engineering, screen arts, music and the written word. Through a series of workshops the aim was to produce a set of 'Learning Bites'; short pieces of electronic learning that could be accessed over the web. Importantly, as well as raising awareness and developing skills with groups who are excluded from IT and online learning, the project has involved working in the environment from projecting lasers on to the water-towers in the East-end to creating drama/soaps. Why I think it is so interesting is that it represents the cutting edge; it is firmly about the creative industries with its focus on the digital, it offers real problem solving opportunities and it breaks down barriers. Additionally, it offered a really interesting, interactive exhibition created by ordinary people using their immediate environment. But most important of all – and this is just in its infancy – it offers a completely new experience for a many people.

7

Design Through Industry

Looking at the shelves in any large bookstore you might be forgiven for thinking that Scotland had only ever produced one designer. With the exception of Frank Lloyd Wright or Antoni Gaudi, few designers have the honour of having an industry created around them. But Charles Rennie Mackintosh is only part of the story. Lionising Mackintosh's reputation might be good for a tourist economy desperately in need of iconic attractions, but despite the recent upsurge in publishing on Scottish art, and despite the fact that we have more design historians than any other country in the world, plenty of interesting designers have been left out. Not least, the industry of kitsch that has developed around Mackintosh's legacy has helped perpetuate the false notion of design as something superficial, whether 'designer label' jewellery or jeans.

The roots of design in Scotland, as in other nations, lie in the craft tradition. For instance, in medieval times Scotland was renowned for its silver work. But Scotland's real design history begins with the industrial expansion of the nineteenth century, when people began to make decisions about what mass-produced goods should look like. At that time millions of yards of cotton, linen and jute were pouring out of the mills of Angus, Lanarkshire and Renfrewshire. The carpet industry in Dundee and Glasgow, the linoleum industry in Kirkcaldy and calico printing in Dumbartonshire supported an army of anonymous artisans.

Where most creativity and innovation was evident was in shipbuilding and marine engineering. In their designs for marine engines, the Napier brothers, David and Robert, combined advanced technology with aesthetics, so dominating world markets. These were the forerunners of the modern designer. But if there is a Scottish identity in design, it is defined largely by Glasgow's industrial history as Second City of the Empire. The influence of shipbuilding and the clustering of crucial resources - skills and knowledge - on the Clyde in the nineteenth century on the following generation of designers cannot be underestimated.

In Glasgow towards the end of the nineteenth century – as in Birmingham and Manchester – design and the crafts blossomed. Edinburgh also experienced a flourishing of the plastic arts linked to a rise in romantic nationalism. There the focus was Patrick Geddes (1854-1932) and his promotion of the coming together of science and culture, and his encouragement to base artistic ideas on indigenous sources. A great deal of design in Edinburgh was narrative and figurative within the pervasive arts and crafts movement. Not being designed for mass production, wider movement was prevented. Glasgow at that time, however, had more than twice the population of the other three Scottish cities combined, with commensurate impact.

There was another reason for the Second City's huge influence. The growth of design and designers coincided with the rise in middle-class consumption and an unprecedented demand for interiors, teashops, fashions and objects to meet their growing appetites. Glasgow Style, that unique version of Art Nouveau, not only satisfied their ubiquitous tastes, and gave Scotland its very own design movement.

Mackintosh was prominent in this, but he was not alone. As a student at the Glasgow School of Art with 'The Four', his wife-to-be Margaret (probably the most important design partnership besides the modern American team of Ray and Charles Eames), Margaret's sister Frances and her future husband Herbert McNair, he worked at the centre of a prodigious design culture. The world of these designers was not dogged by over-production or the unethical exploitation of technology. They were innocent enough to attempt to create a design that celebrated Scottish identity by drawing on Celtic and clan symbolism and to do this in a new way. These designers created a wider market for their work through competitive international exhibitions in Vienna, Budapest and Turin; something that preoccupies today's design and enterprise agencies in an overcrowded global marketplace.

Enhancing industry to give competitive advantage over foreign rivals was around long before the DTI or Scottish Enterprise. You could say design education began in Scotland. In the nineteenth century William Dyce, better known as a painter with the Nazarene group, actively promoted links between science, art, design and craft. As master at the Trustees Academy in Edinburgh he published the first handbooks on drawing, whose aim was improving design standards. He also studied continental design methods at the behest of the Board of Trade and as a result of his efforts was invited to London to help create the national system of Government Schools of Design, whose target was to aid manufacturing industry. Dyce continued a tradition established by the Foulis brothers, who opened one of the first art schools in Europe in Glasgow in 1753. The Foulis Academy built upon Scotland's world reputation in printing, its students providing raw material for a growing industry. The system Dyce set up included schools of art in all Scotland's cities and major towns. Glasgow School of Art had been a government school of design from 1840 and by 1889 seventy-five per cent of its students found jobs in design. Francis Newbery, the school's celebrated headmaster and patron of Mackintosh and his circle, was a strong believer in education meeting local economic needs and training in design as distinct from art and craft. He also welcomed mechanisation and mass production.

Later in the 20th century, it was another Scot, William Johnstone, who took up the baton of a dedicated design education. As well as anticipating abstract expressionism by almost two decades – 'A Point in Time' is arguably the most important Scottish painting of the 20th century – as head at

Camberwell and the Central Schools of Art in London, Johnstone bequeathed a nationwide system called Basic Design, which had a major influence on post-war art school education.

Styles and fashions in both education and design come and go. Art Nouveau, followed by Art Deco, was only to be succeeded by functionalist Modernism, which dominated design culture for the best of the 20th century. Any identifiably Scottish design trait was limited. Bute Fabrics is perhaps the exception as the last remnant of the once-mighty Scottish textile industry. Bute has developed what was a pretty tweedy 1970s collection into a sophisticated palette, using designers such as Jasper Morrison to turn the product into an international brand.

Though manufacturing industry in Scotland has been altered by the silicon revolution, today's breed of new designers thrive in a milieu, a cultural tradition that continues to give access to skills and know-how as well as a sense of identity and purpose. It is also interesting that a country's creativity is often seen to emerge from a sense of contest over identity and what it stands for, usually in the midst of battles between old and new. Both Glasgow and Dundee's efforts to re-invent themselves through culture and to throw off their industrial image to become post-industrial cities are two cases in point; Glasgow with its 1996 International Design Festival and more recently the UK City of Architecture and Design in 1999, and Dundee by Design based in the emerging and culturally successful Dundee Centre for Contemporary Arts. Even in the middle of regeneration, Celtic motifs and Mackintosh still abound, although separated from their symbolist and art nouveau contexts. But there are plenty of present-day designers who not only demonstrate a willingness to break away from Scotland's mythical past but show a positive can-do spirit.

One area in which modern Scottish design has achieved spectacular success is in lighting. From Sydney Opera House to St Paul's Cathedral, famous buildings around the globe have their exterior illumination created by Scots lighting designers. In less than two decades, from a standing start, Scotland's capital city has become home to the world's most renowned lighting specialists; people such as Andre Tammes, Jonathan Speirs and Kevan Shaw. They may be said to have invented modern exterior lighting and transformed the night skies of the globe. Scotland's rise in international lighting design started with Andre Tammes who began work on Edinburgh's Lyceum Theatre before joining up with architect Jonathan Speirs to found Lighting Design Partnership (LDP) in the 1980s. Their business approach was symptomatic of the new Phoenix entrepreneurs. Scotland was to be their base and inspiration but neither the limit of their market or ambition. They were instant internationalists, maintaining a London office and seeking their major commissions in Europe. For last year's Olympic Games, LDP opened an Australian office where Andre Tammes re-lit the Sydney Opera House.

Design is now seen as a way of communicating personal and political ideas, including identity; as a means of exploring social, cultural as well as economic issues; and as a way of changing environments and behaviours. If the approach of our *fin de siecle* engineer and draughtsmen forebears has been lost, it has been replaced by design companies such as Glasgow-based Graven Images. Graven Images is one of the few Scottish companies to have been exhibited at London's Design Museum. The company has curated shows there, as well as designing exhibitions on design for the British Council. As well as exhibition design it encompasses graphics, interiors, products, furniture, architecture. An evangelism about design's multi-faceted role has been promoted by its director partnership, Ross Hunter and Janice Kirkpatrick through broadcasting, research and education. Against the grain, Graven Images has successfully survived the idiosyncratic 1980s and 1990s, and even the PR puff of Cool Britannia. Although based in Glasgow, more than half its clients are outside Scotland. It has now been joined by a coterie of younger companies: textile designers Timorous Beasties, DNA and Squigee; product designers ID8, VK&C and One Foot Taller and a number of other innovators.

In the 1990s, interest in design began to grow in Scotland. Edinburgh launched its Wealth In Design events in the early part of the decade and followed up with the annual Manifesto architecture and design festival. In 1999, Glasgow was UK City of Architecture and Design. These activities helped raise aspirations, but more importantly left a legacy in the creation of The Lighthouse, Scotland's Centre for Architecture, Design and the City. The Glasgow Collection has succeeded where previous initiatives such as the Scottish Design Council failed, by risking funding to allow designers the chance to get their designs beyond the ideas stage. Images of the Glasgow Collection proliferate on the pages of the National Culture Strategy, highlighting a new perception of design. The successor to the Glasgow Collection is now based in the Lighthouse, based in Mackintosh's regenerated Art Nouveau Herald building. The Lighthouse has given Scotland a national focus for design (including architecture) for the first time. Not only has the Lighthouse mounted exhibitions of designers never seen here before such as Phillipe Stark, Dutch company Droog and Norway's Peter Opsvik, it has also given young Scottish companies their first showing. And, its education and outreach programme is continuing the long tradition of Dyce and Johnstone.

8

Burning Questions

While the embers may have cooled in Edinburgh's Cowgate, emotions have not. The flood of words following last month's partial devastation of the Old Town has raised a number of issues about urban life and how it can be sustained successfully. There are at least four inter-connected concerns, each of which demands serious attention away from the heat, post-conflagration.

First, and this is wholly to be expected in the context, is the early tendency to polarise discussion into an architectural contest between Modernists and Traditionalists. The second, which is linked to the first and likewise superficial, is the equating of demands for a contemporary, visionary response with the erection of 'signature' or 'iconic' buildings. Indeed, The Scotsman has been awash with the views of one side or the other. In that sense, issue number three is the way the debate has been conducted as if it were a wholly Edinburgh-centric affair. This is ironic, given the predilection of some commentators to inveigh against the Modernists by underlining the site's World Heritage status. Fourth, and most important, therefore, is the fact that the argument should be correspondingly global in scope; it is the very status of the site that should take the argument beyond Edinburgh and Scotland, and to look at the international community for lessons and examples.

Overarching these is the issue of sustainability, which is central to the manner in which we go about urban development. This is not just because buildings account for 50 per cent of CO_2 emissions and their impact is serious enough, for sustainability goes beyond environmentalism to subsume conceptions of culture and economics. Sustainability is the key idea of the 21st century. It gives us an entirely new way of thinking about the world, including the chance presented by the Cowgate fire, and should force us to think about the effects of our legacy. It implies meeting the needs of the present without compromising the ability of future generations to meet their own needs. It fundamentally affects our concept of urban life.

Each of these emerging issues requires interrogation if a mature and discerning discussion is to take place, especially as historic cities such as Edinburgh grow more and more congested through the combined effect of increased tourism and traffic. Whatever faction one owes allegiance to, it is not simply a matter of making close comparisons based on the restoration of historic centres, or arriving at a novel solution celebrating the contemporary, for the key issue is the sustainability of the Old Town and intertwined with that the amenity of the people who live, work and play there. And, the debate has to be made meaningful to the wider public – it is too important to leave to the architecture and heritage professions.

One thing the newspaper accounts seem to be agreed upon is that architecturally, the buildings destroyed were not in the words of historian Ranald McInnes, 'wonderful in their own right', but remarkable because they were part of a set-piece. What Robert Adam called his 'one connected design' was never realised in the way that he intended (if so its loss would have been utterly tragic) and the buildings flanking the South Bridge were completed by Robert Kay in a much plainer form. So, invoking Adam as part of an argument for restoration might be to over-stretch the point.

Nor is making straight comparisons with other historical cities necessarily helpful. The restoration of Lisbon's Chiado, also destroyed by fire, is surely useful but there is now a wealth of experience from other cities devastated by traumatic events whether through fire, war or natural disaster. 'How People Renew, Rebuild and Remember' – the title of an exhibition showing at the Lighthouse, Glasgow (24 January-14 March) – looks at the experience of eight cities. The processes adopted by New York, Beirut, Berlin, Kobe, Manchester, Oklahoma, San Francisco and Sarajevo are all relevant to Edinburgh's Cowgate. The overriding consensus is that behind the Cowgate's tackiness thrived a rich cluster of small-scale, creative enterprises. Described as a 'soup of uses' and a 'melange', the Cowgate is in actuality what many cities are striving to achieve artificially – a real, live hub for the city's creative industries. Such a concentration is seen as central to the notion of the 'sustainable city' and the Cowgate provided that centre. Surely it is possible to create new, low-key buildings and services for these industries and their users that doesn't merely improve on what was there but reconfigures culture and its creative networks and points the way for all the many cities that will be watching.

Scotland has many talented architects who could fit this bill. Some of the Edinburgh contenders have already set out their stalls, such as Richard Murphy, Ben Tindall and Malcolm Fraser. And there are others around who have successfully pulled off the creation of multi-purpose cultural centres, such as Page & Park and Zoo Architects in Glasgow. In fact, there are numerous Scottish practices that come into the frame and there are leaders in sustainable design such as Bennetts Associates, currently showing at the Lighthouse. Reassuring though this may be, choosing an architect through international competition or otherwise is several stages down the line.

What is more immediate is debunking the notion that creating something contemporary necessarily means producing a 'signature' building – anathema to heritage commentators such as David Black. The Bilbao effect, meaning the demise of the Guggenheim and its exhibitionist brand architecture, according to Deyan Sudjic, has now collapsed and with it architectural hyperinflation. Economy of means, it appears, is once more the guiding aesthetic. Where Scottish architects have been given the opportunity to design landmark buildings, and done this successfully, it has been with the same creative juxtaposition of old and new as deployed by Adam; Page & Parks' respectful regeneration of Mackintosh's Herald building into the Lighthouse and Richard Murphy's carefully crafted Dundee Contemporary Arts being but two cases in point. Being modern doesn't have to mean 'iconic'. Anyway, extravagant, signature buildings no longer fit the sustainability agenda.

Because Edinburgh is, after London, the second largest UK visitor destination, tourism is a major consideration in the debate. Visitors come because of the city's built heritage (although, strangely, the accolade of World Heritage Site has had a negligible effect on numbers). The point is that achieving equilibrium between the needs of tourists and those of the citizens is difficult. Complaints from both groups are numerous, mostly to do with congestion and overcrowding. Busy popular spaces attract the young but intimidate families and the elderly, and incessant street entertainment can make life miserable for workers or residents. There is a lot to be learned from cities such as Copenhagen and Barcelona in the design and management of public space. The re-designed Cowgate should incorporate these lessons and offer relief for visitor and local alike. But more is required; re-thinking tourism is now an essential element of the sustainability mind-set.

Barcelona is hugely useful in many respects. It is looking beyond the short-term economics of tourism and the detrimental effects on the well-being of its inhabitants. Its politicians are well aware of the danger of the city becoming a pseudo theme park and its unsustainability in that sense. In response, Barcelona is developing Ciudad del Conocimiento, The City of Knowledge, based in the former industrial district of Poblenou. Many cities, of course, are declaring themselves to be such. What is interesting in Barcelona's case is the recognition of the longer-term realities and the extent to which it has placed sustainability high on the agenda. New models are being developed in Poblenou, of waste management, bio-diversity, infrastructure and transport, along with ways of integrating university R&D with industry, and culture with economic development. With Scotland's abysmal record in waste management and energy use, and under-performing economy, the regeneration of the Cowgate should be a model of sustainable development and creativity. Being visionary in the 21st century means taking on board sustainability and all that implies. Edinburgh could show the way. Robert Adam would have approved.

9

A Score Created for Frozen Music

National architecture policies and, linked to them, national architecture centres, are much in vogue these days. Indeed, following
on from an international conference held at the British Museum
in 2002, *The Importance of Architecture Centres* will hit bookshops
this year. There is even a European Union text, 'A Resolution for
Architectural Quality in Europe'. There are two points to be
made in this context. First, this activity and the accompanying
flurry of publications is to be welcomed by anyone with an
interest in promoting what has been a hugely under-developed
field – and here I mention the new book Scottish Architecture
2000-2002, edited by myself. But the second is the most
important. A few years ago all of this would surely have passed
Scotland by.

However, devolved Scotland is at a fascinating point in its
history with recent political, social and economic developments.
Architecture is at the centre of this debate. Now, far from being at
the extremity of international events, with the Executive's Policy
on Architecture, The Lighthouse as national centre, membership
of key networks like the European Forum on Architecture and –
because of these prescient developments – with a privileged
place at every conference and seminar, Scotland is elbowing its
way to the front.

Of the several contributors to Scottish Architecture 2000-2002,
writer and critic Caroline Ednie raises the curtain by asking what
the National Programme – a main agency of the Policy on
Architecture – amounts to, exactly. In so doing she defines an
important parameter, whether or not the supposed beneficiaries
of the policy programme are getting value for money or 'what
bang for the buck?' as she puts it. Lest those of a sensitive dispo-

sition fear that consumerism is the sole driver, Ednie is at pains to rehearse the reach of the community dimension and the social diversity of its range. In a country with the depth and extent of social inequality as Scotland it would be unforgivable if a truly national programme on architecture did not seek to involve those most excluded.

Architecture, in terms of the Policy on Architecture, covers more than just objects but includes landscape and urbanism. In constructing an imaginary dialogue with himself, Elco Hooftman, a director of landscape artists Gross Max, succeeds in avoiding the mistake of looking merely at the exceptions. By examining the relationship of landscape and architecture, he surveys the wider scene of Scottish architecture, taking in the Miralles' Holyrood project as well as a variety of smaller initiatives. Hooftman's witty conversation manages to elevate the notion of architecture as an evolving process (Miralles again) whilst questioning ideas of national identity by, quite simply, suggesting an Architecture for Scotland. This should be design-led and involve the young and adventurous.

Hooftman's plea on behalf of the young is amplified by critic and architect Mark Cousins, who highlights a number of interesting young practices and at the same time pinpoints the systemic blockages. How can a small country (but with a disproportionate number of architecture schools and graduates) sustain a vibrant architectural climate and compete in what has become a global architecture market?

Joined-up-ness is the leitmotif of several of the texts. For community architect, Pauline Gallagher this means a fresh awareness of the language of social inclusion. She draws a contrast between this new understanding with all its informal opportunities and the other, older definition with its constrained formality. Suffice to say, this publication and the other elements in the architecture policy constellation are firmly of the former. Sketching out this new knowledge, Gallagher eschews easy analogies to do with the perceived popularity of *Changing Rooms* and *Home Front* and their alleged democratisation, instead focusing on the much more relevant, life-changing reality of Scotland's distinctive claim to having a tradition of participation.

The other important connection is between art and architecture. Neil Gillespie explores how we are moving towards a live culture, which, like the Policy on Architecture, sees 'people, space, art, culture, environment as its expanded field'.

Another connection, in this case between the old and the new, where empathy and dialogue are crucial, is the focus of Historic Scotland Chief Inspector Richard Emmerson's piece. The sensitive fusing of the old and the new is not simply a matter of building technology. It is no coincidence that Emmerson employs the metaphor of the dance - the ultimate in connectedness - to facilitate his description of those recent projects, which have pulled off the delicate task of satisfying different critics and yoking together competing interests. Architecture may be frozen music but it is bloody difficult to choreograph.

Curiously, it is this look at heritage which throws up the most intractable of issues. It is that, in the main, it is the younger generation of architects who are executing the virtuoso performances and having to weave a tortuous dance through planning, complicated funding procedures and converse with all the interested lobbies, whilst the larger firms, usually in tandem with the authorities, progress big schemes with ease.

Although we have gone out of our way not to single out particular buildings, some have permeated the different contributions. Malcolm Fraser's DanceBase is but one instance. The first point to be made is that there are key references, which not only show the way ahead, and indicate that there are things happening. The second is that the Policy on Architecture, being relatively young, can only claim a certain amount of success in this regard. What is certain is that the level of activity shows signs of increasing and that, as well as built objects, this includes all the interactions, conversations and interventions that join-up the built environment.

10

The Limits of the City: Urban Models and the Worldwide Expansion of Urbanism

It is certainly true that market-led globalisation has fragmented and debased the Scottish urban environment, creating what David Page and Miles Glendinning have called 'Clone City' (and this is quite appropriate from the country which created Dolly The Sheep), that is, the product of uncontrolled, mass-produced urbanism, and the problem of unattended 'in-between' spaces. Cloning is the ultimate symbol of regimentation and anarchy at the same time. And, at the heart of the contemporary debate about cloning is the issue of identity. If uncontrolled cloning of animals or humans encroaches upon personal identity, then the city formed by mindless, market-driven forces is a corresponding threat to our collective identity. Cloning relates also to the vast electronic distribution of images and the disputed or contradictory identities they represent. In the case of Scotland this can range from the Edinburgh of Irvine Welsh's heroin addicts to the Edinburgh of Adam and Hume, to Braveheart-type wilderness landscape to Brigadoon romanticised hills and glens. The reality is, of course, quite different.

A geological dig into Clone City reveals a number of fragmentary clues. The most important of these is the realisation that Clone City, or dispersed urbanism, is part of a process spanning several centuries, and represents a to-ing and fro-ing between successive Utopian opposites. From the eighteenth to the 20th century, through the Enlightenment and the making of Neo-Classical Edinburgh to the Industrial Revolution, the unrestrained growth of Glasgow as the workshop of the British Empire to the Modernist New Town and Cumbernauld, with its all-in-one megastructure town centre, it was a powerful stimulus to creativity and diversity. The difference today is that we cannot afford, like Patrick Geddes' rejection of machine based industrialisation or critiques of Modernism or Postmodernism, to undergo another 180 degree turn. However, in Scotland we have seen the return of the notion of the ideal common-place, a hybrid idea that at once suggests ownership and location but also the everyday, the democratic as well as evoking that Scottish Enlightenment idea of common-sense and public sensibility – a common sense of place in other words.

The notion of the common-place seems to have come full-circle back to the competitive private market spirit and enterprise of the eighteenth and nineteenth centuries but without the hierarchy of decorum that gave those periods their unifying thread of collective order and social meaning. This revived market society is a far more fluid and egalitarian one and expresses itself architecturally through the more liberal forms of modernism. The challenge now is to create genuine common-places rather than just icons driven by the ephemeral demands of the market. So, how is this to be achieved? I can only talk through my experience as a director of a national architecture centre. 'Common-place', as a way of resolving the issue of 'in-between' spaces, is for The Lighthouse, Scotland's National Centre for Architecture and Design, a project focussed on the places both intimate and expansive that we occupy with other people; those connecting spaces that are purposeful or unaccounted for. It is an exhibition, publication, website, seminar and education programme.

'Common-place' seems to me to sum up The Lighthouse and what we do in terms of acting as a broker or intermediary agency between the built environment, the professions and the general public. On the one hand 'Common-place' is an exhibition about architecture or non-architecture, if you like, because it is about the spaces beyond our homes, the public spaces that give us identity. On the other 'Common-place' is a demonstration of the role of design in urban and rural regeneration and the irreducible role of local communities in that context. The exhibition consists of nine projects, disparate in size, use and appearance; small shelters, parks, gardens, industrial wasteland and buildings used by groups and individuals, strangers, friends or acquaintances. Each uses architecture and design as a means to create wider connections between communities and marginal places, between the past and the present or between the city and its surroundings. They deal with the minutiae and the meaningful and present a broader view of what the built environment can be defined as.

Public space should acknowledge three kinds of difference. The first concerns ourselves as human beings and accepting that we not all the same, and that people of different cultures, race, class and gender have different ideas about space. The second is physical and the realisation that public spaces should look and feel different from each other – we need all sorts of spaces from the rough to the smooth, the ordered to the wild. The third is the experience we have of space – we need to encounter the familiar and the unfamiliar, to be accepted and challenged at the same time. Charles Leadbeater, a leading commentator on the knowledge economy has written about the need to develop a culture of curiosity and to use the abundance of technology to give free rein to imagination and curiosity. He cites the example of health – finding out about illness has become a huge area for online learning. Architecture and public space should develop a similar curiosity and, for a start, that means breaking down the barriers created by professionals.

The public interest in memorials gives us a clue and tells us something about curiosity about public space when big issues are at stake. The open space for people to explore issues like war, love, and science cannot be managed by anyone but it can be fertilised. People no longer want simply to be consumers, they wish also to be creative actors. Thanks in large measure to digital technology people now have much greater power to make choices. This power should be educated and directed at the built environment and public space.

There is also the issue of globalisation, which is more fluid and complex than pessimists suggest. People are not passive dupes whose lives are dominated by advertising. Instead of homogenising cultures it could be argued that globalisation is spreading cultures through food, art, design, music and architecture. It may be much more profitable to see how we can use globalisation to increase people's awareness and their decision making powers. Clone city came about because the grand utopianism of the twentieth century lay in the hands of a technocratic elite, of planners and architects. Perhaps we should strive for a participative utopianism fed by a global demand for imagination, creativity and innovation. Perhaps we should learn from consumerism and apply the lessons of innovation to public space.

11

Re:Motion and the Scots' Invention
of Mobility

The Scots' Invention of Mobility

There is a strong connection between motion (or mobility), sustainability and Scotland. Why? Scots can lay claim to inventing many of the things that now comprise the world of mobility from roads and bridges to the fax machine. It is not a great leap from these to the systems and structures which facilitate, link or house them – Scottish architecture and planning. Indeed, the Scots' invention of the modern world and the historical development of Scottish architecture are intertwined. In the eighteenth century Adam's neoclassicism was to become the first truly international style in the same way that Scottish-style commercial society was about to become the paradigm for modern capitalism. The two are inseparable and are inexorably linked to mobility. When James Craig and Robert Adam designed neoclassical Edinburgh, what they created, as well as a successful model of urban planning, was a new chapter in modern urban history. But, by developing an environment for a middle class community it replaced the vertical divisions of social class – servants in the attic, well-to-do in the middle and artisans at street level – with the horizontal model with which we are all to familiar, in which the poor are distanced physically and culturally.

The Scottish Enlightenment, with Adam as its main architectural protagonist, created a new cultural landscape, a new mental world. At its centre was not the fundamentalist God of the Reformation but human beings with their physical and intellectual mobility as we understand them today. It is interesting that 50 million people around the world claim some relationship to Scotland, a country of less than 5 million. What is it about the mobility of networks that connects us? It is said that Scotland invented the modern world and our claims to innovation seem more than chauvinistic conceit. The road surface we walk upon was invented by Mr (Tar) Macadam, Dunlop invented the pneumatic tire, Kirkpatrick Macmillan the first pedal cycle, followed by the first steamship and the first helicopter flight. The phone, fax, telephone, television – the very prerequisites of contemporary mobility – were all invented by Scots. We claim our identity with and through these physical objects. By the same token we created depopulation, economic migration, 'Diaspora. Re:Motion', is about these physical and mental mobilities.

Scotland is a remote area of the European Community (EC) and has to struggle for sustainability and relevance in ways smaller countries close to the core of the EC do not. The extremes that have fashioned contemporary Scotland – rapid industrialisation and rural depopulation accompanied by an extensive diaspora then even faster post-industrialisation – have created a unique set of circumstances from which to consider these mobilities. If this is related to our claims about inventing the modern world through the Enlightenment then an interesting dialogue of opposites is established that encompasses remoteness and congestion, population and depopulation, stability and mobility, location and dislocation; extremes which are at the heart not only of the Scottish, but the European, condition.

Architecture and Landscape

In addressing the theme of Re:Motion, one has to touch on the relationship of architecture and landscape because in Scotland they are inseparable. As Elco Hooftman describes, Scotland has a 'delirious topography ... a landscape created by earth, water, heat and ice in a continuous process of erosion, sedimentation, deposition, uplift, folding and eruption'. Miralles' Scottish parliament, presents the idea that the building should be able to reflect the land it represents. The 'borrowed' landscape becomes a generator for building's mental and physical construct. The parliament and its site are symbolic almost of contemporary Scotland. It butts hard against Edinburgh's largely poor working class urban edge whilst reaching out and connecting with the nearby landscape, 'arriving into the city out of the rock'.

Why is it important to stress this? Two reasons. One is that cities cannot exist without movement. They develop on the back of large inflows and outflows of people, goods and the vehicles and systems that carry them. In Edinburgh, the very city that bequeathed us urban dislocation through the distancing of its new and old towns and the horizontal segregation of its social classes, the parliament can be seen as a form of aggregation, re-connecting the city to the geology that created it, lending greater social cohesion. The second is that this is a theme permeating the exhibition and preoccupying the minds of its contributors with the need for a more sustainable relationship between land and community, city and countryside, history and the future.

Re:Motion: Example

By way of example – the Highlands and Islands of Scotland, whether because of their remoteness or serene beauty, are a source of fascination for many people. Although a tourist desti-nation, they are depopulated as communities, raising issues of sustainability and reminding us that their eighteenth and nineteenth century inhabitants were amongst the first economic migrants. They left their marks on the land they left – the routes they walked, the stones they quarried, and the places where they worshipped. For millions of Scots real or virtual, these are potent, emotional images. Perhaps what is needed is a new kind of visitor centre to service migration in reverse. It has been said that philosophy is really homesickness, the urge to be at home every-where. Maybe visitor centres are the architecture of homesickness. Nonetheless, once crude and architecturally insignificant, visitor centre design is now anything but – the best examples of this relatively recent building typology are highly sophisticated, distinctive, architectural responses – icons of a new mobility. In Scotland, not only has the visitor centre, that new focus of pilgrimage, come of age but is a focus for sustainable design. It is interesting in that sense that Bennetts Associates, one of the most environmentally aware practices in the UK, designed the Gateway Centre, the symbolic portal to the Loch Lomond National Park.

Conclusion: Bringing it all Back Home

This paper is, of course, based on a conceit, that Scotland invented the modern world; that the Scottish Enlightenment bequeathed us the tools and objects of mobility. It facilitated economic migration on an industrial scale but it left us the modern problems of urban sprawl, dislocation and, of course, sustainability. Re:Motion's message is that the future lies in utilising the objects and tools we know; not inventing new ones. It means revisiting older schemes and reinventing them in the light of experience whether Edinburgh or Cumbernauld New Town or the ecologically sound ways of former living in the Scottish Highlands. Crucially, it is about new, imaginative and sustainable ways of integrating and respecting landscape.

12

Patronising Places

The starting point for this paper is the First Minister's 2003 St Andrews Day speech, which laid out a vision for the future of Scotland's culture and economy with a new priority given to high quality spaces and environments. It discusses the significance of the speech and the opportunities for architects it presents. It advances a culture shift from Public Art to Public Design and the strategic role in that process of The Lighthouse as National Architecture and Design Centre.

The First Minister's St Andrew's Day Speech

Scotland's patron saint and environmental improvement are not exactly synonymous but after the First Minister's St Andrew's day speech that could change. Nestling in amongst Jack McConnell's widely reported vision for Scottish culture, especially his declaration of cultural rights for all, and bypassed by most of the media, was his promotion of the entitlement to an aesthetically pleasing environment. 'The planning system can be a powerful tool to encourage creativity in both open spaces and the built environment,' stated McConnell. Whilst the media were quick to relegate the speech to the status of 'social inclusion gone mad' or 'touchy feely arts for all', what they missed was the fact that to support his argument for cutting across ministerial portfolios to deliver his all-encompassing vision, McConnell went out of his way to cite as an example Scotland's first ever planning policy 'Designing Places' and the role of culture in that regard.

With that speech the contribution of design in contributing to a high quality environment, a sense of place and place quality took on a new and sudden, public importance, and with it an unprecedented opportunity for Scotland's architects. What the First Minister said was slanted to the role of art and creativity generally, but his specification of the planning policy in that context cannot be underplayed. For Scotland's built environment to engender a sense of both place and identity as desired by the First Minister requires a culture change of major proportions. Artists have a role to play in that sense but that is not what is necessarily at stake. Attaining high quality environments is not about the elevation of artists in the planning process, fascinating though McConnell's interest in creativity may be. Nor is it necessarily to do with architects and urban designers working with artists. The real issue is design. Indeed, what we need is a culture shift from Public Art to Public Design and an understanding of what aesthetics means in that particular context and in the wider sense of cultural rights.

This paper indicates several ways to secure an irreducible role for design and design professionals within this new vision for Scotland. It does this by interrogating some of the assumptions and misconceptions surrounding the St Andrew's day speech, especially the poorly understood notion of design. The paper also looks at how non-professionals view environmental design. As well as delineating the role of The Lighthouse as National Architecture Centre, it also seeks to illuminate the debate by pointing to some really good, recent examples and in the process define what constitutes successful Public Design. Lastly, the paper sets out an agenda for urban change, which places design professionals at its heart.

Cultural Policy: But What Does Culture Mean?

Having a clear understanding of the relationship between the arts and culture is crucial if one is promoting the roles of architecture and design, especially in terms of the Scottish Executive's review of Scottish culture strategy heralded by McConnell on St Andrew's day. Culture encompasses a wider range of activities than the arts, that assemblage of performing and visual arts also now codified into the cultural and creative industries. This paper acknowledges that there is and should continue to be a widespread and serious debate about politics and culture, and that this discussion reaches globally beyond devolved Scotland. Nevertheless, to remain focussed on the issue of place design raised by McConnell, the paper straightforwardly asserts the role of architecture and design in both cultural policy and as a major element of the creative industries. In this way it allies architecture and design with art whilst differentiating art from the former because of their important economic as well as cultural importance.

A comprehensive view on environment, health, education and economics permeated by art and creativity as advocated by McConnell, is really a conceptual way of integrating disciplines to provide a perspective on complex cultural relationships. Again, it is not the function of this paper to interrogate the St Andrew's Day Speech in its entirety, rather to claim an expanded role for architects and other designers. Nonetheless, the inclination that economics, education, health, environment and culture are interconnected and could be improved through the arts cannot be dismissed. The question may be whether the arts are up to it or whether they should be up to it at all. The power of art lies in its otherness, its ability to defy logic, to subvert, to symbolise, to create metaphor, to vacillate, to dilly-dally. Not least, there is a tendency, certainly in government speak, to treat each of the arts as if they are instrumentally the same when in fact they are markedly different in purpose. This becomes evermore important when discussing space and place because in this instance it is the visual arts that are involved. So, if the visual arts are to be applied to securing environmental quality is that not a commodification of artists' practice, a perversion of art's purpose?

In a post-modern sense it has been widely stated that cultural language is notoriously imprecise. Words like 'creativity', 'art', 'arts' and 'culture' are treated as if they are interchangeable. The critic Terry Eagleton thinks that it is time 'to put culture back in its box' because the term has been so misused as to be irrelevant. One thing is certain, if we are to make a 'Smart, Successful Scotland', we need to employ a more effective common language. One way to effect a culture change would be to stop talking about culture when what is really meant is the arts; another would be to stop talking about the arts plural. Furthermore, instead of art and the environment it would be much more effective to talk about design.

Public Design

At the moment design in Scotland is a problem not a solution. It is poorly understood and lies low down the political priority list. It is seen either as a technical process linked to planning or architecture, an area of activity like graphics or textiles, or simply a superficial label or veneer. It is symptomatic that we are still having a debate whereas our European competitors have moved on. Part of the problem is the failure of design professionals to explain that design is a generic, strategic process that encompasses problem solving, aesthetics, functionality and effectiveness. It can improve lives and environments just as much as it can advance prosperity and economic competitiveness. This failure is one of the reasons for the apparent political prioritisation of art over design.

Former director of the Glasgow 1999 UK City of Architecture and Design Festival, Deyan Sudjic has described how in the recent competition for the memorial for the victims at Ground Zero abstraction and minimalism has become the language of the monument. The progenitor of this was Maya Lin who won the Vietnam war memorial competition when she was an architecture student at Yale and who has set the trend for the past twenty years. Sudjic indicates that, like Maya Lin, none of the eight Ground Zero finalists can be called an artist in the normally understood sense of the term. His point is that they are filmmakers, set designers and architects, professionals who can respond to the stringencies of the brief and the consultation process demanded by the Lower Manhattan Development Corporation. As Sudjic reminds us this kind of thing is customarily called Public Art but given the exigencies of this kind of competition it is nearer to architecture, and it is probably better to describe it as design.

This trend can be traced across the world and, as well as being evident in the context of high profile memorials, can be seen in smaller scale projects closer to home. Glasgow's Reidvale Housing Association, which has won numerous prizes and accolades for its highly successful design approach, has eschewed figurative public art for abstract schemes incorporating, for example, lighting design and more architectural statements. Doubtless this is due to the need to fulfil the spatial demands of social housing and the concomitant need to consult with the tenant clients. What is becoming evident in these global and local examples, where large amounts of public funding are involved, is a greater engagement with due public processes that are sometimes painful, not least because public funding comes with strings attached, often in the form of obligations to respect and meet both aesthetic criteria and public responsibilities as well. For all that, in the case of this housing association, as evidenced in the Lighthouse-curated exhibition 'Anatomy of the House' (2002), video interviews with tenants of the Graham Square development provided an illuminative evaluation that was overwhelmingly positive about its spatial design and environment.

This is difficult terrain for anyone, architects and designers included, but is especially problematic for artists whose priority is creative self-expression. To lead the way through this difficult territory requires an expanded set of competencies beyond the purely artistic as well as the orchestration of competing needs and responsibilities, especially if individual cultural rights are insinuated into the mix. It has also been argued that art cannot handle social or political ideas and in a post-modern sense moves in its own zone. Therefore, when issues of environmental sustainability and improvement are at stake, it would seem that design may be the more appropriate strategy.

Give Me Shelter: Examples from a Small Country

What is also missing from the debate – and schools of architecture could play a much bigger role here – is any serious research on what constitutes quality in terms of public spaces and environments. Post-occupation evaluations are particularly lacking. The most concentrated collection of research abstracts in the field collated by Norskform, the Norwegian architecture and design centre, which contains a comparative analysis of professional and non-professional responses to environmental aesthetics, concludes that there is an outstanding need for real life studies, and that the questions far outnumber the availability or novelty of the answers. In that absence the role of The Lighthouse as national architecture centre assumes a particular public importance in identifying and promoting projects deemed to have made an impact of some kind. Annually, with 150,000 visitors, over 30,000 participants in outreach activities and, monthly some 20,000 website hits, The Lighthouse is in a unique position to perform an intermediary function between public and profession, profession and public.

The Lighthouse has developed a singular, partnership-based, research model centred on the process of exhibition making. It involves a range of qualitative methodologies from digital diaries to video ethnography. In common with the curatorship of other exhibitions it subsumes a wide range of scholarship in terms of art, design, architecture and social history. The outcomes of the investigation are harvested and assembled in the exhibition, which is a very public form of dissemination to a broad audience. In addition, the exhibition format is enhanced with a constellation of other information sources to sustain debate: web site, catalogue, conference, press articles. The Lighthouse model is one therefore that aggregates value.

For example, 'Common-place', the second touring exhibition in a series curated by the Lighthouse and supported by the Scottish Executive's Policy on Architecture, examined nine different projects from around Scotland. One of the high profile projects was Sutherland Hussey Architects' An Turas shelter on Tiree, selected when just a work in progress. During the exhibition's tour An Turas received numerous accolades, narrowly missed winning the Stirling Prize and was championed by Guardian architecture critic Jonathan Glancey as the building of the year. As well as demonstrating that Scotland can produce high quality architecture, albeit of the small-scale variety, the project showed how artists, enthusiasts and architects could collaborate to create something that is widely applauded. Yes, An Turas is an example of art and architecture collaborating but without the design skills of Sutherland Hussey Architects it would never have happened.

A similar case in point is the Campbeltown Wind Shelter which also featured in 'Common-place'. This again developed from a collaborative model with a strong education emphasis and involved a number and range of local groups. Eventually four teams of architects, locals and artists submitted ideas for a design that would enhance the local environment. Artist Calum Stirling's Windshelter with landscape design by Greg White is the result of real community co-operation. Like An Turas this could be read as an environmental art project but the methodology behind the realisation of this project of realising the project centres on design. In this sense the artist is one resource amongst a number. It is how such resources are marshalled and deployed that is salient.

The Lighthouse has accumulated a number and variety of projects which, as well as modelling a novel form of research, demonstrate high quality outcomes whether to do with creative collaboration, community involvement, consultative development processes, well-researched solutions, good client relationships or aesthetic appeal. In all of these there is evident a meta-strategy, a way of integrating aesthetics, planning, co-operative working, research and development, realisation and reconciling competing interests. In other words, design.

Cultural Rights: A Design Entitlement

In these projects The Lighthouse has also interwoven education and life-long learning and possibly a new way of engaging in culture and economic regeneration in an innovative way. What if, as well as (or instead of) visiting plays, concerts and galleries, a cultural entitlement for young people meant participating at some stage in their school careers in a real-life environmental design project in which problems of aesthetics, planning, and consultation were to the fore. And, what if such an entitlement also involved working with architects, designers and artists in the way promoted by The Lighthouse. Every single Scottish youngster attends a school or lives in a community whose sense of place and identity and environmental quality could be to some extent enhanced or would not be harmed in the slightest way by being the focus of even suggested prototypes for improvement. The real-life contexts are limitless as are the opportunities to apply a wide range of knowledge and skills in realistic ways. Would not such an enterprise vitiate the introverted curriculum of Scottish schools and help displace the stultifying lack of creativity brought about by the past two decades of bureaucratic educational reform?

The First Minister has also provided a new 'take' on access and excellence, which are often subject to political trade-off. According to McConnell 'excellence should be accessible and access should be to excellence'. In terms of the arts this piece of word play could fuel endless discussion or cynicism, equally. However, in the context of offering the built environment and the planning system as an authentic context for learning as proposed by this paper, excellence is about the quality of the interaction between student and design professional. In this case the Lighthouse, in its project management role, is the guarantor of quality.

Establishing an Agenda

This brief paper has argued for the prioritisation of design as an *über* strategy in the realisation of public spaces and environments given the new importance attached to the development of high quality environments in the First Minister's St Andrews Day Speech. There may be a globalising trend that would appear to support this direction. Whilst agreeing there is a role for art and artists it has been demonstrated that where artists work in a team to a design master-plan which can orchestrate a stringent brief, handle demanding consultation and facilitate community partic- ipation, the results have proved to be more sustainable, if that is one measure of success.

Nonetheless, if the Design opportunities held by McConnell's speech are to be seized a number of things need to be addressed. Based on the real-life studies undertaken by the Lighthouse as part of its national mission the following might constitute and agenda for action. What is needed includes:

• New ways of speaking about the development of pubic places and spaces; a common language, which can be used by a range of actors. This means, as well as avoiding professional jargon, jettisoning the imprecision of political culture speak.
• New ways of thinking about cultural rights and entitlement that introduce the idea of multi-disciplinary,

cross-cutting environmental design projects, especially for young people.

- New networks with an open architecture that allows greater permeability, introduces new skills and knowledge and allows different people to interact.
- New models of research that utilise new and old technologies, accommodate local aspirations and needs, and convivial methods of public dissemination. Most of all they should encourage experimentation.
- New emphasis on Public Design as a strategy that marshals and deploys resources whether these resources are human, economic, cultural, material or environmental.

Lastly, maybe we need, like St Luke, the patron saint of artists, a patron saint for design. St Andrew sounds the ideal candidate.

13

The Lighthouse and Scotland's Policy on Architecture

Architecture Policy and 'Ready-made' National Centre

When, in 2001, the Lighthouse was awarded an annual grant by the Scottish Executive to take forward a national programme of activities linked to the development of Scotland's policy on architecture, two mutually supportive sets of objectives came together. In the words of the deputy minister with responsibility for architecture, Scotland was fortunate in that it had a 'ready-made' architecture centre in the Lighthouse, with a 'wealth of expertise and excellent facilities'. The targets of the national programme – consistent with policy – were to mount exhibitions, promote community development, stimulate initiatives through an innovation fund and create a virtual architecture centre, while at the same time producing cross-cutting, on-line learning material on the built environment for the National Grid for Learning (NGFL). All of this chimed together with the work the Lighthouse had set in motion, from its inception in 1999 when Glasgow was UK City of Architecture and Design.

Creating the Platform

As well as mounting a series of UK 'firsts' – for example, exhibitions on MVRDV, on multicultural aspects of contemporary architecture and design and debut shows for young Scottish architects and designers, the Lighthouse had, since 1999, been assiduously nurturing a nationwide education and community programme. This was based around three awards for three years: a grant from the National Lotteries Charities Board (now the Community Fund) to develop outreach; funding from the Scottish Arts Council Lottery to get architects (and designers) into schools; and support from the Heritage Lottery to promote a Mackintosh interpretation programme. In turn, these large-scale schemes attracted collateral support from Glasgow City Council's education department to deliver out-of-school activities, and from Scottish Enterprise to progress novel learning experiences for disenfranchised young people.

A New Narrative for Architecture and Lifelong Learning

This case-study weaves together four interconnected elements of the above to show how the national programme and the Lighthouse's own programme converge, and how an architecture centre can not only open up architecture to a wide audience but also become a major content developer and producer of lifelong learning materials. It also demonstrates how these resources are embedded in a variety and range of communities and constituencies. This is quite a different role from that of architecture centres elsewhere in the UK or abroad. The Lighthouse sees architecture as a set of educational, social, cultural and economic concerns, which affect everyone. Thus, it does not focus on the needs and interests of the profession as being necessarily paramount but sets out to look at users and professionals as co-equals.

Case Study: Democratising Exhibitions

Exhibitions are important tools and for three years we have been trying to make the annual Glasgow Institute of Architects (GIA) exhibition much more accessible by innovating its design and presentation. Traditionally, the exhibition included architects like Alexander 'Greek' Thomson and Charles Rennie Mackintosh. The 2001 exhibition was designed by Glasgow-based Chris Stewart Architects, who created an installation that provided an exciting environment in which visitors could submerge themselves, as opposed to baffling displays (for the average visitor) of drawings and models. New building projects became animated images; and a fantastic website projected into a well was surrounded by seating affording visitors the opportunity to fax their opinions to the practices involved with the exhibits as well as vote for their favourite buildings. Attempting to make this annual exhibition more engaging has involved an ongoing dialogue with the GIA, who have been wholly supportive of our inspiration to involve the public with architecture through exhibitions, workshops and other means.

The Scottish Executive fund the Lighthouse to develop an annual touring exhibition and the principles enunciated above infused 'Anatomy of the House'. This exhibition received 25,000 visitors at the Lighthouse and toured Fraserburgh in the north of Scotland, the Edinburgh festival, the Borders and the Western Isles. It is also hoped to take it abroad. The show will have been seen by about 100,000 people, and over five years the exhibition programme will touch half a million people, many of whom will have their first experience of architecture. 'Anatomy' looks at the evolution of the domestic house in Scotland through a number of themes – croft, castle, urban, suburban, settlement – and draws on contemporary examples from across Scotland. It also has a series of satellite events: a conference on housing, raising the issues of how people can be moved from suburban to urban design; how we can stop building rubbish; and how housing might be put back on the political agenda. There are master classes and workshops with housing associations and architects, and an educational pack for schools that was distributed through teachers' evenings. In this way many thousands more will be introduced to architecture and have the opportunity to have their interest enlarged. Over five years we will be monitoring the impact of this exhibition, just as we do other programmes.

From Water Towers and Websites: *Scottisharchitecture.com* and *Buildingconnections.co.uk*

Chris Stewart Architects are also involved in a long-term project focussed on the large water towers that dominate and serve Glasgow's peripheral housing estates. This has become a large-scale environment improvement scheme drawing in people from the communities who live by the towers as well as students, schoolchildren and artists. Essentially, the project is based on workshops that encourage the community to use lighting design and sound-responsive lasers to transform the towers by creating spectacular events. These radically alter not only the environment, but also the awareness of the participants by opening their eyes to what can be achieved in creative partnerships with architects. We also harvest the knowledge gained in such projects.

The Lighthouse is innovating an educational website partnered by Scottish Enterprise. It is couched in the digital inclusion agenda and targeted on disenfranchised young people, but it uses architecture – based on the experience of the towers project – as the stimulus and motivation to develop much-needed skills within the area of the creative industries.

Developing community participation and wider public awareness in the way described above is crucial to architecture policy. This is why a key element of the national programme is the creation of a virtual architecture centre – scottisharchitecture.com –featuring contemporary and historic material on Scottish architecture, architectural tours, discussion forums, architectural practice of the month and information on urban and rural design. All of the community and other initiatives sponsored by the Scottish executive's architecture policy are documented on this site. In turn, this large-scale resource is complimented by another website, *buildingconnections.co.uk* funded by the National Grid for Learning (NGFL), which we think will be the largest anywhere devoted to providing cross-curricular educational material on architecture for schools and colleges. Although targeted on the curriculum in Scottish primary and secondary schools its lessons are transferable to other educational contexts. Its core resource, the built environment, is commonly available to any user. What is important is that for the first time, an ongoing, coherent, progressive resource on architecture has been assembled by educators working with architects, for five to sixteen-year-olds.

Architects in Residence and Getting Architecture into the Community

Architects in Residence in Schools is a scheme run by the Lighthouse that has put a hundred architects and designers into schools and involved over 4,000 primary and secondary students. The projects have ranged from modest schemes to the more ambitious. 'Canal Connnections' was centred on the Millennium Link, which opened in 2002 uniting the Forth and Clyde Canal with the Union Canal to form a navigable route through central Scotland, linking the centre of Edinburgh to the centre of Glasgow. 'Canal Connections' involved 400 design students from eight colleges and universities across Scotland, who developed projects for the Millennium Link Canal according to their own fields of study as architecture, graphics or three-dimensional design. Students worked with community groups and others concerned with the canals to identify real issues and design problems. The project ran during the academic year 2000/01 and culminated in an exhibition at the Lighthouse. It paved the way for the community aspect of the national programme, which seeks to create novel ways of involving the community.

Another example under the community remit of the national programme was a project called 'Pigeonhole City' involving the Lighthouse and GLAS (Glasgow Letters on Architecture and Space). Students were invited to submit proposals for an intervention that would be left in, or become part of, a space or building forming a messaging system on architecture, its issues, events and objects. The brief asked the question: 'If not a website or a building, what can an architectural network be?' The competition was judged by Cedric Price, and the architect of Edinburgh's Dancebase Malcolm Fraser. The wining entry was the 'black book' by MPF (Missing Presumed Found) an anonymous entry. Black books have 'read me' on the front and are left in places fro people to find. Finders are invited to 'use this book as your own for a short time, record your surrounding, take photos, sketch a little and write something too' then leave it for the next person to read and add to. All books are to be returned to the Lighthouse on completion. They have been translated into fourteen languages to be released globally. The development and story of the proposal became an exhibition at the Lighthouse as well as a documentary case study on *scottisharchitecture.com*. Overall the community initiative is committed to developing five programmes each year, the intention being to achieve geographical coverage and involve different communities. In 2001, for example, we ran a large-scale project in Campbeltown, Argyll. Several architecture practices worked with the local community, looking to regenerate spaces. In a more urban context we worked with the *Big Issue* on homelessness and are developing a prototype production machine for cardboard shelters. This rural/urban pattern will continue.

Innovation and Stimulating Demand

Last, central to the promotion of policy, is the Innovation Fund. In March 2002 eight projects were selected and spread around Scotland. Like other aspects of the three now five-year national programme, the Innovation Fund does not set out to support new building; rather the emphasis is on creativity and new ways of working. It encourages built environment-related projects that generate interest through new initiatives and activities. The aim is to promote a network of people and ideas and, in line with the policy, encourage participation throughout Scotland. Projects range from setting up an architecture centre in the Borders through turning a derelict area of Edinburgh into a play park and mounting architecture workshops for school students to publishing a quarterly newspaper on architectural issues, with the emphasis on transforming the environment. The intent is, over time, to create a mass of interested and informed people who in turn will become part of an improved architectural climate.

Conclusion: Ready Made for its Purpose

Growing an audience for architecture should be the primary objective of all architecture centres. This audience, moreover, should not simply be consumers of architecture and the built environment, they should also be 'engaged in matters affecting the built environment' as the policy states. This is not simply an adjunct to other issues that are central to policy, namely, better procurement and improved design quality in rural and urban planning. The social and educational priorities of the policy and its programme are essential in privileging design issues generally. Having an architecture centre, ready made or otherwise, is vital to this purpose.

14

Design Defines the Century

Over the twentieth century various attempts were made at defining design, a process over which many different interest groups have claimed hegemony. In the case of spacecraft, aircraft, weapons, and ships it has always been seen as a matter of specialised technical expertise, most-times anonymous. Only in the case of fashion, cars, furniture and luxury goods has design become associated with individual personalities and even hero figures, and efforts to define it in terms of regional difference and national identity are a relatively new phenomenon. In terms of the consumer, design is governed by polls, surveys, focus groups and more recently the demand for differentiation and customisation. Nonetheless, it is marketing and the power of the brand that holds sway. Does any of this matter in the twenty-first century? Can we define design in a way that is relevant for the new century that does not begin with technology, or with artefacts, nor their creators, appreciators, users or consumers?

In English, design is both a noun and a verb, referring to intentions and plans as well as fashioning and concocting. It is also connected (and this tells you a lot about the English language) with deception and cunning. Craft, which too is a noun and a verb, has as its adjective crafty, also meaning cunning. According to the philosopher Vilem Flusser, designers are like cunning plotters because they bridge art and technology to overcome or deceive nature. However, this is not to open up a sterile semantic or philosophical debate. Rather, the point is that at the beginning of the twenty-first century we are better able to see behind artifice or trickery. Our education and access to communications technology means that we can interrogate for ourselves claims about 'weapons of mass destruction', the inequities or benefits of globalisation, ethical or environmental matters linked to industrial development, or issues relating to our identity. What we are seeking, it would seem, propelled not only by the likes of pressure groups, eco-warriors, and global protestors as well as other post-industrial changes, is the perfect reconciliation of needs with resources. What was previously concealed, whether by design or accident, is now subject to greater debate and analysis – the process is a matter of wider public concern. Thus, design has become a matter for a broader constituency. In that widened context it is also important to consider design's other connotation, its relationship to sign: a sign of the times, a sign of things to come, a sign of membership. In other words, everything now depends on design. It is its role as a bridge between technology and art, ideas and ends, culture and commerce that is now important, not in its surreptitious twentieth century form but in the openness of its twenty-first century definition.

This collection of papers seeks to open up design's expanding range; a selection of key figures in the European design field discuss a number of inter-connecting themes. Peter Zec sets the scene by underlining how innovation and social structure have to intertwine in order to create the climate needed for survival, far less sustainability. Indeed, describing what the future needs to be like and choosing the correct direction to get there is a function of leadership – a key element in the new arena of design management - and is at the core of Raymond Turner's contribution. Taking up that leadership challenge requires the application of a business tool and according to Jan Stavik, design proffers such a tool. Luisa Collina and Giuliano Simonelli underpin Stavik's thesis by underlining the importance of 'design driven' innovation. The debate is amplified by Steiner Amland who indicates how design is now integrated with other contexts and thus sets another challenge – designers need to re-evaluate what they do in that light. All of this is congruent with the contemporary re-defining of design, however, with that convergence come certain responsibilities.

Crucial to this re-definition, re-evaluation and re-emphasis and the responsibilities embedded therein, is the issue of sustainability. This is developed through the contributions of Peter Butenschon, Ezio Manzini, Karen Blincoe and Francesc Aragall, all of whom agree that it is the design profession that should take the lead on the issues of sustainability, Corporate Social Responsibility (CSR), and Design for All. In this sense, if there is an over-riding narrative, it is that design has emerged as an inter-connected economic, socio-cultural and environmental concern with wide-ranging relevance to the citizens of Europe. Certainly, much of the foregoing discussion refers to cultural as much as it does economic change.

This progression is nicely encapsulated by Jordi Montana for whom design should move from being a dialectical process with manufactured nature (the cunning plot) to being a dialectical process between people and cultures in permanent communication with nature. This is a way of grounding design in the local ecology and thus, of propagating regional identity. To be successful, and this is Johan Valcke's point, design promotion has to recognise this and be organised locally, in order to promote local strengths more effectively. The subterfuge of Scottish electronic products with Japanese names or Flemish fashion branded Italian is no longer sufficient for more demanding and discerning European consumers, who can see through the 'plot'.

In this more transparent context, values, another twenty-first century concern, therefore can be communicated more honestly. Helmut Langer believes that as visual culture grows designers are the key brokers in transforming information into knowledge and values in that sense will strengthen European identity and competitiveness. Importantly, he highlights the difference between globalisation and homogenisation; globalisation means a multiplication of values. Fundamental to these values ecology or family of responsibilities - especially the relationship of ethics, sustainability and design – is education. Design education, no less than the design profession which informs and which it is informed by, is also subject to a host of economic and social pressures. In Europe this is particularly acute due to the Bologna Agreement and the likely convergence of education systems and curricula, and movement of students. Like the design profession, education requires to overhaul (re-design?) itself to relate to future needs. In that context a number of those needs are identified by Norman McInally; promiscuity, ego and play are added to some of the characteristics McInally believes necessary to attain the desired flexibility and transferability, and which, in some degree, design already possesses. Indeed, from Robin Edman's viewpoint, design thinking should be integrated across the higher education curriculum to pollinate creative alliances essential for future growth. Paola Bertola concurs with this view this the production of new knowledge is key, advocating that research should become a permeating, continuous process for both business and academia. In that sense, design requires to be put higher up the academic research agenda.

Of course, the concerns of this White Book are not confined to Europe; they are universal. To take but one example; the South Koreans are actively developing a design policy that embodies many of the issues set out here. As Michael Thomson reminds us, the South Koreans are only one country in Asia amongst a number who are embarking on similar initiatives. Even if there were no other pressures illuminated by the contributions to the White Book, the encroachment of Asian countries into areas hitherto assumed to be the sole territory of European design creativity, in addition to their march on Western manufacturing and service industries, would be reason enough to raise the matter of a European policy, or at least a resolution, on design and its promotion. It is hoped this White Book will provide the components of such an increment.

15

The Great Heritage Con

TV programmes such as *Restoration* give a false impression. Not everything from the past is worth saving. In each hour-long programme three buildings (representing one geographical area) are selected for salvation by public vote and this year's Scottish entries which feature this week certainly live up to the programmer's need for evocative, threatened old ruins: a falling down castle; the derelict home of a former explorer; and a working but dilapidated old mill; would all seem to fit the necessary bill for nostalgia and romance. Portencross Castle in Ayrshire, Orkney's Hall of Clestrain and Knockando Wool Mill, Morayshire, are the Scottish Stars in this heritage drama.

Neil Ascherson claims in his book *Stone Voices* that the relationship between Scots and their geology is so intimate that they 'form a single cultural landscape'. Poetic perhaps, but if the stones that make up the country's architectural heritage industry are anything to go by then Scots are just as uniformly obsessed by the past as the rest of the UK. The way *Restoration* treats the issue of threatened historical buildings – seeing them as if they were an event, and their conservation akin to an act of religious charity – is to present the heritage industry as unquestionably a good thing. But is it?

The heritage industry – a relatively recent concept dating from the early 1970s – has now become so powerful that having a view of old buildings which is anything other than saving them (far less knocking them down) is not politically correct. Having an alternative is not to deny the particular merits of the three Scottish examples nor the potential community, educational or touristic benefits that may or may not arise from their refurbishment. The point is that programmes like *Restoration* with their isolated focus on single buildings and their histories (and the more romanticised the better) miss out the wider context. Apart from trying to invest architecture with a *Changing Rooms*-type mentality, they give a distorted view of urban or rural design. For urban or rural planning is complex and a fuller public understanding of architecture needs to be developed in order to participate in the debate. Note that *Restoration* does not raise critical questions; it simply presents buildings as a series of interesting stories with the most compelling securing its own future.

There is of course, the other extreme. Some people believe that the fascination we have with old buildings is morbid, pathological even. It would be healthier, goes this version, to demolish old buildings and start afresh. Finding the saner, middle ground is difficult. The argument in the press after Edinburgh's Canongate fire, which quickly polarised into conservation versus modernisation, is but one recent example.

If you ask yourself the question, 'should every old building be saved?' you immediately arrive at the heart of the matter. Apart from not being sustainable environmentally, economically or socially, because the question avoids how people and the ways in which they live and work have changed, it also prevents a whole-hearted engagement with the future. Creating the built environment we want for ourselves should not be reduced to a question of demolish or save, conserve or modernise. In recent years Scottish architects have demonstrated how you can incorporate a respect for the past with a desire for the future – Edinburgh's Dancebase and Glasgow's Lighthouse are a couple of outstanding examples of this in practice. The simple fact is that some buildings are worth saving and some are not. Which category Portencross Castle, Knockando Woolen Mill or the Hall of Clestrain come into is eminently debateable. Restoration aside, there is a real debate out there just waiting to happen.

16

No Place for a Public Hanging

The reviews of the new Scottish parliament building in the professional architecture press have – with minor qualifications – been overwhelmingly positive. None, however, has seen fit to mention the art bedecking the interior walls of the building.

Indeed, what is uniformly remarkable about those reviews is their focus on the artistry of the architecture itself. Never has the word 'poetry' been used so much in the analysis of a building. Ellis Woodman, writing in Building Design, summed up Miralles's designs as 'uncommon poetry'. For Neil Gillespie in the *Architect's Journal*, the building represents an act of imagination bringing together 'politics and poetry'. For Deyan Sudjic in *Architecture in Scotland*, it is a 'delicately wrought romantic poem'. And the *Guardian*'s Jonathan Glancey was moved to describe the structure as 'magical'.

What is art for? The question has been asked down the ages. Certainly art is more fashionable and popular than ever, and debates rage about its accessibility or otherwise. But what art is good for in the context of the parliament building is an entirely different matter. It seems to have stirred little debate, as if it were a fait accompli when, in fact, it could be seen not only as a violation of the design aesthetic of the building but an obstacle to a wider and much-needed discussion about design in Scotland.

Miralles's big poetic idea was to create not a building but a landscape into which he could embody the complexity and romanticism of the Scots identity, and which would simultaneously reflect the growth of the democratic ideal. It is a building, therefore, that overflows with imagery, iconography, symbolism and metaphor.

From Le Corbusier in Chandagar to Norman Foster in Berlin,

it is something that every architect in the last century charged with the gargantuan task of designing a parliament building has sought to achieve. Whether, according to your view, Miralles was a romantic maverick, hedonist or visionary, all of the professional critics are agreed that he was undoubtedly the architectural artist of his generation.

What is also certain is that the parliament building is full of art – sculpture, drawing, design – all of it Miralles'. It is the only building in Scotland for years, maybe since Mackintosh's School of Art, that might justifiably be called a Gesamtkunstwerk, a total work of art. So why is it necessary to fill it with quite alien wall-hangings, photographs, sculptures and paintings, setting up in the process a totally unnecessary contest between art and architecture?

That there have been more column inches in the Scottish press about the parliament's art than its architecture is down to the fact that no Scottish newspaper employs a professional architecture critic. Therefore, by default, there is a totally one-sided conversation. It has even been suggested that the fact that the artworks are difficult to place in the parliament was the fault of the architect for not creating sufficient space for art. Thus, there is a double failure – an inability to recognise and celebrate architectural quality and a diminishing of the Scottish parliament's undoubted power to express the complexity of our national identity. Every architecture critic in the UK gets it. Why not the Scottish art lobby and our parliamentarians?

It could also be argued that architecture such as Miralles's has obliterated the difference between architecture and art. More importantly, architecture today is filling the space abandoned by contemporary art by offering exciting, creative objects such as Foster's Gherkin, Gehry's Guggenheim or Hadid's Riverside Museum, which appeal to a global audience. The reason that architecture is so much less hyped than art is because architects are less glamorous and architecture is as much a commercial as it is an aesthetic concern. Also, when people talk about having more art in the parliament they mean visual art. Why not, like the Flemish parliament, have exhibitions of contemporary design or, like the Canberra parliament, proudly promote it as a showcase of Australian design?

However, there is a problem with contemporary visual art. Despite its fashionable success, it is a source of consternation, because it tends to veer between two extremes. One is that art needs no justification, the other is that art should serve a clear purpose, especially where pubic money is concerned. This is exacerbated by the fact that much contemporary art is conceptual and shrouded in arcane discourse. Accommodating art in that sense, therefore, becomes extremely difficult and specialised, and there is a need for a lot more mediation between artist and spectator. Is that really the job for a parliament with a part-time curator?

It is not that the artworks in the parliament are bad or that there should be no art at all – they might be appropriate for some of the offices and smaller meeting rooms. The issue is that they are, for the most part, superfluous. They certainly do nothing to enhance the interior. In fact, in most instances they detract from the real art – the parliament building and its exquisitely crafted interior.

In comparison to Miralles's architecture none of the artworks on show can quite stand up to the determination of his design. The bottom line is that the building was not intended for such extraneous artworks and Miralles was quite clear about what should and should not go in the building, the furniture included. At the heart of this is a well-intentioned but misguided notion about the role of art in public spaces. The debate about Percent for Art and the relationship between art and architecture has been well rehearsed and is well understood – if not in practice, certainly in theory. That debate emerged out of the context of post-war architecture and the perceived exclusion of artists, linked with a move to get art out beyond the gallery. However, this is not to say that every single public building needs artworks dotted all over it, especially in the case of the parliament, which, as Sudjic puts it, is haute couture architecture.

The parliament is not an art gallery. Uniquely, it houses a diverse and imaginative set of Scottish signs and images, from the tilted St Andrew's cross embedded in its concrete to the iconography of the black granite panels which symbolise the balanced movement of Raeburn's skating minister and act as a metaphor for democratic debate. There is also the use of light that accompanies the image of leaf-forms and upturned boats, moving in procession to the giant leaf-form of the debating chamber, creating a luminosity that is quite outstanding alongside recent European buildings.

Perhaps what is needed is more appreciation and interpretation of the architecture. Clearly there is a demand to satisfy the needs of the many hundreds of thousands of visitors who appear drawn to the building. The unprecedented visitor numbers not only counter the potentially debilitating effect of the Fraser Enquiry but confound the notion that architecture is for the elite few. There is a huge public demand for the appreciation and enjoyment of architecture – the parliament has demonstrated this, and reaching for words such as poetry, magic, imagination puts it in the sphere of great art. This also brings in beauty and aesthetics – ideas with which the public can connect.

This huge manifestation of public interest also suggests that the parliament is more than just a building, extraordinary though it is. It clearly points to architecture's newly discovered ability to engage with people's imagination and thinking at a number of levels. The fact that this is happening in Scotland is remarkable and should be seized as the opportunity to address the public's current disaffection with politics and invigorate the debate about democracy and citizenship. This needs to be done in engaging and innovative ways. There is a role for art here but an even bigger role for design and designers.

Design is central to achieving high-quality buildings, but design is also a practical tool that helps to make things more visible, legible and coherent. A new way to think about design is as a process that puts users at its heart and works from their perspectives. Good design in that context is no longer simply about style or producing new objects; it can also be used to ensure 'user-friendly' interfaces that improve public services. The advent of the parliament and its success should stimulate a Scotland-wide debate on the need for high-quality design to pervade all aspects of Scottish life, including the design of better communication between government and people.

A building as complex and demanding of critical attention as the Scottish parliament does not require artworks, far less an artworks policy as indicated by some commentators. The last thing we need is for it to become a repository of Scottish art – Scotland already has plenty of art galleries. It would be great, though, if Scotland's artists, designers and architects did engage with the parliament, stimulating a fresh debate about art, design and architecture and what their role in contemporary Scotland might be.

We have a world-class, iconic parliament building; let's keep it that way.

17

Designs on a Budget

Amongst the hundreds of pages in the recent Budget statement, you might be forgiven for missing Gordon Brown's very interesting intervention into the UK's creative industries, particularly design. As well as usefully underlining the importance of creativity to business success right across the UK economy, especially the 'impact of product innovation and design', the Chancellor announced a series of measures – steps to increase the contribution of creativity to productivity growth. These included inviting Design Council chair, George Cox to undertake a review to ensure that SMEs apply creativity and innovation to improve performance and are able to draw upon the UK's world leading creative skills in areas like 'product and industrial design...graphics, branding and advertising'. Cox is someone who is sceptical of governmental reviews but changed his mind because of the importance of the added value creativity can bring to business and his belief that government has come to realise creativity's importance to UK competitiveness.

The budget statement also encouraged the English RDAs to consider how best to integrate design into corporate strategy, product and market development through the Design Council's Design Immersion campaign. The North of England is given special attention in terms of the launch of a modern Design Centre in Newcastle/Gateshead to ensure that businesses are able to access creative talent and design skills. All of this is to be underpinned by research – in a further measure aimed at accessing the creative sector's substantial capability, the DTI are to help firms to identify how creativity can improve their performance. And, by the by, the Chancellor also provided £12 million to develop commercial and business skills in the cultural sector.

Apparently, at one level, this is great news for the UK's design and creative industries and a triumphant outcome of the Design Council's discussions with the Treasury. At another level, it raises questions about the role of design, creativity and innovation in post-devolution Scotland because none of Gordon Brown's measures relate directly to circumstances north of the border. Design does not enjoy the same priority in economic development terms here as it does south of the border, far less the investment outlined in the 2005 Budget. Yet, with well over two thirds of Scottish companies failing to failing to generate new products or services, the lack of creativity and innovation is a major threat to competitiveness.

Certainly, in Scotland, through Scottish Enterprise, there is an emphasis on developing the creative industries and recent studies reinforce their importance, especially their concentration in Glasgow where design is particularly strong. However, the Treasury's focus is not the creative industries themselves, but how more of that creativity can be deployed within manufacturing and how the sector's strength can magnify its impact in mainstream business. Through its nationwide Creative Entrepreneurs Club, The Lighthouse has been proactive in promoting connections between the creative industries and other sectors like the Medical Devices industry as well manufacturing. It has also established particular training initiatives: Creative Collaborations is a programme of workshops, which brings together creative industries and SMEs to share information, examine potential partnerships and create a pool of knowledge. The strength of Creative Collaborations is the evolution of a collaborative network. It is widely reported in innovation research that strong, managed collaborative networks are a stimulant to innovation. Coincidentally, another initiative, the Creating Growth programme, addressed the development of the managers from the creative industries, particularly their leadership characteristics, well anticipating the Chancellor's support for this area.

The Lighthouse has also been proactive in promoting Scottish designers and architects abroad, a fact recognised by Jack McConnell, the First Minister. Scotland has a tremendous record of design creativity and innovation. Our designers and architects are used all over the world. We don't lack creativity; what is lacking is the creative thinking that will embed innovation across Scottish business and industry.

There needs to be further support to provide opportunities to connect SMEs and creative industries. Design and the creative industries act as a lever of innovation across all industrial sectors and advantage is achieved through recognition of that fact as the Chancellor has so clearly stated. Structured network development, with clear learning, business and economic development outputs is required in order to facilitate not just the development of the creative industries, but also their recognition as a lever of innovation within other sectors. Whilst The Lighthouse has taken a national lead in that respect much more needs to be done. Taking heed of the Chancellor's measures to use design and creative industries to stimulate business growth and challenge our competitors would be an important step.

18

Welcome to their Space

Why isn't the general public more interested in contemporary architecture? Tuned into interior makeovers, are blobs, shards, pods and vegetable shapes a turn-off for the present-day audience? Take Archiprix International – the world's biggest student architecture competition. Archiprix gives us the privileged view of world architecture seen through the eyes of students. At one level it shows great delight in form-making and spatial design and glancing across the range of projects Archiprix exhibits is that rare quality avoided by much contemporary art – beauty. But on another level Archiprix shows a real respect for place and place-making. Importantly, Archiprix demonstrates that architecture is now re-occupying its former territory – aesthetics, form, content, context.

In a sense, Archiprix is like holding up a mirror to what is going on in the architecture world. Architects are now designing some of the world's most interesting sculptures – they just happen to be buildings. And, student architects are no exception. However, this is not to suggest that students are slavishly following global trends. Sure, there is evidence of the sophisticated image-making enabled by more and more powerful software – the technology that makes fantastic structures possible. But what is really interesting is how students across the world are using these as tools to come to terms with complex issues. Not only is this allowing them to reach beyond the superficiality of much contemporary practice but also to use architecture to re-invigorate visual culture. Students, like some of their professional peers, have discovered that you no longer have to design flashy buildings to get attention. Showiness is out; seriousness is in. The participants in Archiprix are clearly engaged in a conversation that is wider than narrow professional concerns, and rightly so.

In Scotland, the location for Archiprix 2005, there is as elsewhere a fear of the perceived failure of 70s Modernism – McMoMo™. The claim is that the fundamental ideals of the Modern movement have been corrupted and mutated by McWorld into mechanisms of commercialisation and alienation. Even in the country that could be said to have given birth to global capitalism through Adam Smith's *Wealth of Nations*, this is simplistic, and for the critically challenged, just too handy an argument. By holding up a mirror to practice across the globe Archiprix shows that this debilitating narrative can be challenged. Archiprix is not simply a reflection – it is a vantage point. The world that students look out on is complex, nuanced and diverse. In that sense, their work behaves like cultural probes; continually prodding, jostling, poking, uncovering, discovering.

Interestingly, the subversion of technology and the return to a much greater stress on investigation of socioeconomic and other issues has happened alongside a rekindling of interest in building and construction. This is a change in direction from earlier Archiprix competitions. Whether this is a clearly identifiable shift is debatable – there is still no apparent loss of student interest in transitory landscape or fragmented urban situations. Yet, in this particular context, an emphasis on the section and attention to detail, instead of merely underlining technical practicalities or prioritising structural concerns over design, answers the need for realisation, for a coherent programme, for an architecture in the fullest range of its meaning, as well as heralding a return to figuration. Maybe this is what it means to be an emerging architect in the first decade of the twenty-first century.

By its very nature, being simultaneously recherché, eclectic, ethical, restless, local/global, inclusive, today's student work resists straightforward categorisation, more so than in any previous decade. What can be picked out though, is a determination to utilise the tools of design not as part of a reductive, instrumental procedure, but rather as a broader cultural strategy. This is where it is easy to confuse the contemporary student preoccupation with different modes of presentation – painting, photomontage, collage, and digital media – with a cosmetic, desultory approach that merely tries to imitate the idioms of present-day art. To do so would be quite wrong. These are processes of enquiry that extend design thinking, fit quite comfortably within an enriched range of methodologies, and reaffirm architecture's vital role in visual culture today. This is a phenomenon that allows aesthetics, emotion and figuration to co-exist with an interest in sustainability and a sense of place and identity.

The important point here is that an audience exists for the diversely rich activity that Archiprix International encompasses. That audience has a hunger that is not assuaged by the intentional emptiness of much of contemporary art. The great thing about architecture – and the generic term 'the programme' is wonderfully expressive in this regard – is that it has got both content and context, both process and product, as well as a sense of inter-connectedness. It cuts across social, economic, political and cultural concerns so it touches everyone. Design is the connective tissue. Archiprix International represents all of this and more. It is not just a student competition; it addresses a fundamental, universal demand – to understand more about how design can help us make sense of and improve the increasingly confused world in which we live.

19

Glasgow Design City

The Nineties: A Virtuous Circle of Creativity

Whether your abiding memory of the last decade is Diana or the Dome, Retro or Reality TV, it was in the Nineties that we learned to love our old industrial cities. What became a global phenomenon – the post-industrial transformation of cities by design and cultural regeneration – is the mark of how Glasgow, through its reign in 1990 as European Culture Capital, used design to define a decade. The timing was crucial. Helped by Roger Hargreave's graphics and the marketing acumen of its civic leadership, Glasgow, once the Second City of the British Empire, commenced its long and painful journey from the gloom of its industrial past with Glasgow's renowned 'Miles Better' campaign in the mid-Eighties and one of the biggest urban ground shifts in history.

With its associated inward investment and cultural strategies – the Garden Festival, the opening of the Burrell Collection (a landmark building predating Bilbao's Guggenheim by a decade) – that campaign secured the 1990 European City of Culture crown and created a virtuous circle of design creativity, including the 1996 International Design Festival, leading to the prize of UK City of Architecture and Design 1999 and the opening of the Lighthouse as Scotland's Centre for Architecture, Design and the City. So what about the role of design in terms of Glasgow's past, present and future as the Nineties as a 'Design Decade' gives way to more recent notions of the Creative Industries and the Creative City?

Three Pillars of Wisdom

There are at least three prevailing pieces of wisdom about the impact of design and cultural developments on Glasgow in the Nineties. There is within these an inherent cynicism that I am sure would transfer to other cities. The first has it that City of Culture and ensuing design-led initiatives had little effect – at most 6,000 jobs were created in the creative sector and most of these were temporary. The second is that 1990 sparked off a renaissance in the city's economic regeneration by creating a platform for the emerging Creative Industries – media, design, architecture, and music – set up by a growing army of cultural entrepreneurs.

The reality is that elements of both those stories are true. The third 1990 story is that repositioning Glasgow as a City of Design amounted to more than hype. Sure, it did not solve all of the city's problems but, most importantly, what it did do was drive a process of adaptation and self-learning in which the city (in other words the public sector), with the private sector, sought to develop Glasgow's cultural assets and develop its creative economy. This is very important in terms of differentiating between cause and effect relative to today's debate and the emergence of Richard Florida's 'creative class'. There is another important aspect in sorting hype from reality and cause from effect, that is, design's actual impact and role within the process of regeneration over the more generic role of the arts.

In a serious sense – certainly in the case of Glasgow – that debate began in earnest with Design Renaissance, the International Design Congress staged in the city in 1993. It marked a moment when designers stopped showing each other pretty pictures and started talking about more far-reaching contextual issues coming to bear upon their work. Indeed, predating Florida by ten years, Janice Kirkpatrick, a Glasgow designer declared that investing in people – rather than iconic – projects was the way forward. Also significant was the fact that artists were beginning to emerge in Glasgow as important not just for enhancing place quality (that is a by-product), but for delivering stinging (and sometimes unwelcome) critiques of urban regeneration – with it went the recognition that this in itself gave Glasgow an edge as a creative city.

However, if any help is needed in this exercise then one only has to try to envision what the city would have been like had there been no investment in Glasgow as a City of Design – the outcome, quite frankly, is unimaginable. In fact, Glasgow has been a model, with its momentum-building techniques copied elsewhere in Europe. The place marketing that started with the Glasgow's 'Miles Better' campaign and was the multiplier effect in City of Culture carried through to the 1996 and 1999 city design festivals did focus strategy on narrowing the gap between hype and reality. It also projected Glasgow as an innovative city. It has certainly earned a 'can do' reputation as developments in design and the visual arts demonstrate.

What other city in the past decade has launched what, in its time, was the largest performance and exhibition space in Europe with Tramway (1990). The transformation of Tramway from industrial to contemporary art space has been widely copied, most recently by the Palais de Tokyo in Paris, Friche in Marseilles and Baltic in Gateshead. Tramway was recently revamped at a cost of $6 million. What other city has opened a Gallery of Modern Art (GOMA) which attracts half a million visitors a year? The recent $15 million rehabilitation of the Centre for Contemporary Art (CCA) consolidates Glasgow at the cutting edge of the contemporary art scene. But, and this relates to the need to understand how strategies are promoted, the provision of physical spaces goes hand in hand with artist-led or 'soft' initiatives – exhibitions, of course – but also non-gallery and public art projects, magazines, records, posters, prints, graphics, flyers, graffiti, DJ/VJ s, demos, clubs, talks, readings, polemics. And, for example, relative to the size of the city, Glasgow artists have trumped their rivals in the UK national Turner and Becks awards as well as gaining international exposure. These cultural assets not only enhance the visual arts but they are crucial in attracting and retaining Richard Florida's 'creative class', that new breed of designers, architects and artists who, in Leadbeater's words 'create wealth from thin air'. This offers a contrast to earlier, failed examples of event-led urban regeneration focussed solely upon physical manifestations, of which international examples abound, not least in North America.

Glasgow UK City of Architecture and Design

One of the most important staging posts for Glasgow as Design City was its reign on the eve of the Millennium as UK City of Architecture and Design. Described by one national newspaper as a 'shimmeringly successful year', it attracted over 1 million people to its exhibitions, 40% of whom had never been to an exhibition on architecture or design before, and thousands more took part in education and community events. As well as events there were actual build projects – Homes for the Future – an innovative mixed private and social housing project in a historically deprived area of the city; and a project called 5 Spaces, which set out to achieve a sense of place in pretty inhospitable territory. All of this; the exhibitions, events, and other projects, put a lot of investment into the design community in terms of commissioning design, graphics, exhibitions and buildings – 50% of design companies in Glasgow believed that their turnover would increase as a result of the festival. Importantly, in terms of industrial design, there was also a hard-nosed economic development project – The Glasgow Collection – which sought to promote innovation by subventing the costs of developing new products and encouraging emerging graduates to stay in the city. In fact, because of the combined capital and revenue investment of £27.5million ($68.75m Canadian), the impact of Glasgow 1999 was closely evaluated and was reckoned to have generated £60million ($150m) as well as the indirect impacts.

The Legacy: New Models for Culture and the Economy

Developing a reputation for innovation linked to the creative economy has accelerated with the Lighthouse – the $25 million conversion of Charles Rennie Mackintosh's former Glasgow Herald building – to Scotland's Centre for Architecture, Design and the City, and the $40 million Science Centre on the former site of the Glasgow Garden Festival. Both projects demonstrate a continuation of the change mentality. As well as being about cultural tourism they also sit on the crossover from cultural consumption to cultural production, design being the connective tissue that joins up science, technology and art. The Lighthouse especially, with its mix of exhibitions, events, education, design into business and creative industries' network, is on the commercially active side of the arts-economy equation – what is in the UK termed the Creative Industries – and is establishing a new business model and tools for the design sector. This, in a sense, is one of the real legacies of the Nineties. Also, research about what a design museum for the twenty-first century could be like has highlighted the value of The Lighthouse as a design centre that has created a distinctive local identity but which, at the same time, is located in an international context.

Creative Cities and Creative Industries

Commentators like Richard Florida – but also in the UK people like Leadbeater, Bentley, and Landry – have grown careers talking about the creative economy and the importance of place in sustaining cities. However, the development of Creative Industries, inexorably linked to sustainable city development, emerged as a UK government priority in 1998 and has been a strategic focus for the devolved Scottish government since 2000. Indeed, Scotland's First Minister recently called for Scotland to become universally recognised as a 'creative hub'. The Creative Industries is one of the fastest growing areas of the UK and Scottish economy. At a UK level they are worth over $200 billion and account for over 5% of GDP and at a Scottish level, $17.5 billion employing 150,000 people in a country with a population of 5 million.

Importantly, in terms of the urban context 10% of these jobs are in Glasgow. Even more interesting, according to a very recent publication on Creative Industries, Glasgow has the largest share with strong concentrations in film, TV, publishing and cultural industries, that is, galleries and museums, but also the strongest design base outside London. More recently, *Time* magazine rated Glasgow the new music capital of the world – 'the new Detroit'. Recent research has posed the question as to whether having such a concentration of creative industries is accountable for the strength of the international visual arts culture, or the so-called 'Glasgow Miracle'. In other words, in Glasgow, design, perceived as the invisible thread that permeates and interconnects architecture, publishing, music, software, games, is maybe responsible for the vigour of its cultural community, which, in turn, is responsible for attracting other categories of people and investment. To put it another way, it is design and the Creative Industries that are indeed the cause and not simply the effect as described by Florida. The point being that design may be playing a bigger role in urban regeneration than commentators have previously given credit.

City Strategies for Design: Lighthouse for Design

Nonetheless, this concentration creates a rich urban ecology, which is bilateral in that it enhances both place quality and improves competiveness. Certainly, the design-led festivals and other cultural initiatives of the Nineties in Glasgow aided this advance, but it was accompanied by large-scale public realm and capital investment projects. And, in line with Florida's thesis, it was also accompanied by grassroots visual arts phenomena. The Lighthouse is the physical manifestation of this, intersecting both national and local governmental policies and strategies. For example, The Lighthouse underpins the delivery of Scotland's architecture policy, acts as a network hub for the nation's Creative Industries, promotes internationalism, and is currently heavily involved in the development of a design strategy with local and national dimensions.

Central to the latter are the issues of talent creation and retention, creative business development and innovation, design promotion and international networking. Specifically what this means is that, as well as showcasing local design talent like Timorous Beasties, textile designers whose work is in the collection of the V&A and the Cooper Hewitt National Design Museum in New York, we take exhibitions abroad to places like the Milan Fair and the Venice Architecture Biennale. It means networking on a national and European scale – we run a Creative Entrepreneurs Club for professionals and students through which we offer advice, training and support and doing things like developing digital educational materials for pupils in schools colleges and universities. In other words, The Lighthouse aggregates value by promoting design as an interconnected social, educational, cultural and economic concern transecting both public and professional groups.

Collaborations

The Lighthouse transects local and national strategy on design and partnership is a key element in that sense. One example is a multi-layered collaboration with the National Endowment for Science Technology and the Arts (NESTA). NESTA has commissioned a major piece of research into the Creative Industries, a major finding of which was the necessity of greater collaboration between investors, the public sector (including education) and creative entrepreneurs. Key to that was 'investor readiness' amongst young or starting-up designers and design companies. Thus, The Lighthouse is involved with NESTA on several projects: Insight Out is a mentoring scheme targeted on recent design graduates of Glasgow School of Art that aims to develop them and take their ideas to market. IdeaSmart is a high-risk fund which also includes a range of partners and, as well as offering grants to designers, gives collateral support in terms of advice on business planning, marketing and presentation. The Graduate Pioneers Programme, although UK wide, is supported by Lighthouse and aims to take the very best design graduates in the UK, and to nurture, harvest and distribute their ideas. At the same time, NESTA supports The Lighthouse's Creative Entrepreneurs Club, a networking scheme that aims to focus collaboration within a pretty disparate sector comprised largely of SMEs (very small – medium sized enterprises), who operate solo or as freelancers.

What all of these collaborative initiatives point to is the need for:

- Graduates and businesses: knowing what is possible and what is expected of them.
- Investors: understanding the real commercial potential of early stage creative businesses.
- Policy and decision-makers: recognising the significance of partnerships, sectoral intelligence and leadership for a growing Creative Industries sector.

Creative Hub

New strategies are being formulated in Glasgow, which take cognisance of the development of the Creative Industries and the interconnection with the Creative City as posited by Florida et al. These take the form of five key themes:

- Creative infrastructure
- Creative business
- Creative workforce
- Internationalisation

- Creativity and innovation

In terms of infrastructure, a Creative Industries Hub is proposed in Glasgow's Merchant City, its former warehouse area, currently undergoing a physical and symbolic transformation into a creative quarter. There is also a need to provide specific business support and in that sense the role of the Lighthouse is changing to take on specific account management of design/architecture practices, which for a design centre is an evermore-interesting meld of culture and business. New kinds of training and professional development have also been identified which require new forms of educational brokerage to offer a sustainable ladder of support – The Lighthouse's work with NESTA and academic partners is one instance of this approach.

Internationalisation is central to the future strategy. This year (2004) The Lighthouse has taken exhibitions to the Milan Fair, London's 100% Design, the Venice Biennale and Utrecht and Marseille. As well as creating routes to market for designers, these events have a critical role to play in promoting the city and the image of Glasgow. Critical also is nourishing creativity and innovation and in that sense partnerships with academic research institutes is of extreme importance especially in terms of what knowledge transfer in the Creative Industries is all about. However, most important is inculcating an environment in which creativity and innovation can flourish. For a post-industrial city like Glasgow on the edge of Europe this means avoiding parochialism by showcasing design and architecture talent from elsewhere and this is where an architecture and design centre such as The Lighthouse performs a singular role by staging exhibitions and events that draw on the best of what is going on around the world.

Summary
Over the twentieth century various attempts were made at

defining design, a process over which many different interest groups have claimed hegemony. In the case of spacecraft, aircraft, weapons, and ships it has always been seen as a matter of specialised technical expertise, most-times anonymous. Only in the case of fashion, cars, furniture and luxury goods has design become associated with individual personalities and even hero figures, and efforts to define it in terms of regional difference and national and urban identity are a relatively new phenomenon. In terms of the consumer, design is governed by polls, surveys, focus groups and more recently the demand for differentiation and customisation. Nonetheless, it is marketing and the power of the brand that holds sway. What is salient is that cities – and Cities of Design is one indicator of this trend – are now being discussed in the same terms. Does any of this matter in the twenty-first century? Can we define design in a way that is relevant for the new century that does not begin with technology, or with artefacts, nor their creators, appreciators, users or consumers?

Nonetheless, in the creative economy it is uniqueness and innovation that ultimately will be the key. It is these things that make Glaswegians as unique as Londoners or Milanese and Glasgow as intriguing as Barcelona or Montreal. Glasgow European City of Culture 1990 spun that identity and can rightly lay claim to kick-starting the rise of the creative city.

20

Better by Design: An Architect Who Truly Deserves His Iconic Status (Charles Rennie Mackintosh)

When does an icon become an icon? Some buildings, like the Bilbao Guggenheim, achieve iconic status from the moment they are built. Others, like the Glasgow School of Art, take years. Completed in 1909, it took half a century for it to attain iconic status. At a time when cities are in global competition, employing international architects to give them instantaneous iconic buildings, Charles Rennie Mackintosh's School of Art trumps all those two-minute wonders and wannabe icons. A real landmark, it shows how buildings don't have to be flashy to be noticed.

In an age of architectural hyperinflation when blobs, shards, gherkins and seemingly endless towers jostle for our attention, the School of Art and its playfully inventive design stand out. It has been described as a 'youthful' building. Mackintosh was a young man when he designed it and it shows his many enthusiasms whether architectural history, buildings he sketched on his travels, or what was going on around him in the design powerhouse that was Victorian Glasgow. The building's originality comes from the free-play of those different influences and interests – an inventiveness that has the worldwide, popular appeal essential for iconic status.

The Art School is undoubtedly an icon of world architecture but Mackintosh's own iconic status is based on a breadth of innovative architecture demonstrating the variety of work that was open to an architect in the Empire's 'Second City'. From the *Glasgow Herald* (now The Lighthouse) and *Daily Record* newspaper buildings to Scotland Street and Martyrs Schools to Queens Cross Church and The Hill House in Helensburgh,

Mackintosh's energy and creative range is still outstandingly evident.

Why is Mackintosh's work a wonder? Like his European counterparts, Mackintosh was trying to invent a new style but his was based on the Scottish vernacular. He used Scots baronial architecture, tower houses and other native references in his work. Gaudi in Barcelona, Hoffman in Vienna and Horta in Brussels were also pioneering a similar vision of a national architectural style combining decoration and structure. Thankfully, because of the contemporary phenomenon of the blockbuster international touring exhibition with its extensive media coverage, people have rediscovered Art Nouveau and discovered Mackintosh. Because of this he has found a prominent place in a highly popular art movement. People can now see that he was not a lonely genius but one among many celebrated designers – a connection that the international trade in cultural tourism has readily exploited and helped consolidate Mackintosh's iconic status.

Mackintosh was also youthful or innocent enough to attempt to create a design that celebrated Scottish identity by drawing on Celtic and clan symbolism. He did this in a way that was new but not parochial, and merited widespread international attention. Mackintosh is wonderfully unique because he was that rare thing, an artist, architect and designer all rolled into one; a creative industry before the term was invented. The School of Art and his other buildings like the Hill House are masterworks because they successfully integrate structure, decoration, interior design, furniture, lighting, artwork – they have everything going for them. Even his commercial tearoom interiors show the same sense of artistic unity. Most present-day architects or designers when they think they are artists turn into egotistic attention-seekers and usually produce self-indulgent design and second-rate art. In contrast the School of Art and Mackintosh's other buildings are examples of icons that really work. The Art School, in continuous use since it was built, is about to benefit from major investment, The Hill House has been lovingly conserved by the National Trust, The *Herald* building transformed into The Lighthouse and the tearooms are being lovingly restored, whilst his for House for an Art Lover took shape nearly 100 years after it was first designed. All have become major tourist attractions. The iconic status of Mackintosh's work flowered late but it is now synonymous with Scotland as a creative nation.

21

6000 Miles

6000 Miles is the fourth in a series of touring exhibitions developed as part of the National Programme in support of the Scottish Executive's architecture policy. *6000 Miles* continues to broaden public awareness of architecture and the built environment and promote The Lighthouse's aim of creating exhibitions targeted on a wide audience. At the same time, it seeks not only to innovate exhibition making in terms of novel curatorial approaches but also, in the process, engage with a broad spectrum of people.

Exhibitions on architecture tend to be either historical one-liners or concern themselves with celebrity architects and iconic buildings. They also tend to be isolated, self-referential one-offs, focussed on a narrow, primarily professional, audience. *6000 Miles* and its predecessors run counter to that trend. They constitute part of a coherent, continuous programme that is rooted in a national policy that sees architecture as a wider public issue, transecting culture, economics and society. Moreover, *6000 Miles* sets out to demythologise, to open up architecture and the built environment, to invite a diversity of viewpoints, and so expand the debate.

6000 Miles is the distance around Scotland's coastline. But it is not simply the length of a jagged contour; it literally shapes our identity and delineates our image of Scotland – it is topology and iconography, both. It is a point of entry and departure. It is margin and edge. It differentiates us from our continental neighbours, culturally as well as geographically. Scotland's coastline is also a site of contest – of industrial revolution, degeneration and then regeneration, of migration and asylum and of religious and political settlement and upheaval.

How we have interacted over time with our coastal landscape and waters and the physical transformations that have been implemented, is the context for *6000 Miles*. The exhibition is not purely historical. It explores a range of scenarios and interrogates specific sites. This questioning approach is aims to contribute to the debate on the future usage of Scotland's coastal areas by providing a series of proposals – ideas that can be modelled and developed into real-life projects – targeted on five themes:

- Production and Transportation
- Leisure and Consumption
- Energy and Environment
- Weather and Time
- Work and Habitation

The investigation, which is team-based and collaborative, draws on the skills of architects, designers and artists as well as the expertise of naval and maritime practitioners, and continues the action research-based approach established by previous exhibitions. In *6000 Miles* this has been taken even further through the innovation of the Coastal Machine – a metaphorical engine capable of encapsulating the changing social and environmental processes that might impact upon our coastal regions over the next half century. The choice of machine is a conscious one, as opposed to the exhibition convention of static building or installation, and is in tune with the notion of coastal activity and constant motion.

This catalogue documents the research process and as such represents a useful contribution to the very slim literature on the development and contemporary relevance of architecture exhibitions. Importantly, this documentation, an illuminative evaluation in every sense, is put into a historical frame of reference linked to each of the five themes. Thus, the Coastal Machines – the output of the investigation of the five teams, are appropriately contextualised and, hopefully, capable of wider application.

6000 Miles seeks to democratise architecture and the built environment in two ways. First, it provides a subject and content relevant to the needs and interest of the enquiring citizen that is neither dumbed down nor exploitative. Second, it offers a means of participation, of engagement and enjoyment – using this catalogue and its processes anyone can undertake an investigation and interrogate their immediate local environment as a means of understanding and managing change. Lastly, by seeking to democratise architecture *6000 Miles*, simultaneously offers a conduit to the democratic process and to identity politics.

22

When is a Designer not a Designer?

When is a designer not a designer? When she has just been announced as Designer of the Year by London's Design Museum, apparently. The award of the accolade and prize money of £25,000 – the design world's equivalent of the Turner Prize – to Hilary Cottam who is director of Red, a Design Council thinktank, has stirred up an unholy row amongst the normally discrete, black cotton suit brigade. It's a debate that is interesting in several respects, not least because it reflects the changing world of contemporary design, especially at this time when the Chancellor, Gordon Brown has just commissioned Design Council Chairman George Cox to undertake a review of the UK's creative industries and their potential to support the performance of British business.

Cottam, who would never claim to be a designer anyway, beat off stiff competition from the likes of Glasgow textile designers Timorous Beasties and industrial designer Jasper Morrison. The newly acclaimed Designer of the Year is one of a new breed on the design scene; someone who acts like a film producer – a project champion, fundraiser and manager all rolled into one. But people like Cottam don't produce things in the conventional sense; they provide a catalyst to make large-scale things happen, in this case the environmental and social transformation of a run-down school in southeast London to become a high performing institution. As well as involving teamwork, this requires political nous, coupled with the ability to proselytise design as a creative problem-solving activity that crosses economic, social and cultural boundaries. Cottam has done similar work on prisons and her current work at the Design Council centres on the reform of public services through the transformative power of design. As a former employee of the World Bank, Cottam is a brilliant spokesperson for the economic, as well as social, benefits of such schemes, as well as being an outstanding advocate for design. The prevailing world economic view that innovation and technology are synonymous is changing. According to John Thackara in his new book 'In the Bubble', innovation starts with groups of people who have the tools to connect with each other, and who can identify and secure resources in order to co-ordinate actions between people, actions and places. Thackara believes that the challenge for designers is to work out how they can address this trend. But designers alone cannot solve all the world's problems. Given the scale and complexity of the social, economic and technological challenges we face, perhaps what is really needed is a new form of design manager or animateur – someone who understands how to orchestrate the move from designing for, to instead designing with people to make the world a better place. Cottam fits that bill.

However, when visitors to London's Design Museum were asked to choose between Timorous Beasties' printed textiles, Morrison's product designs, and Cottam's Kingsdale School, the assumption was that she, like the others, was a practising designer. Selecting her, some say, is like giving an actor of the year award to Steven Spielberg or the Turner Prize to an exhibition curator. The complaint from many people, including the Kingsdale's head teacher and the project architects, was that not only was she not the designer, but that she usurped her role to steal the limelight. Nonetheless, that Design Museum visitors chose her based on her school project instead of much more sexy designs demonstrates a step-change in public perception. That there is a contemporary audience for design fuelled by the popular media goes without saying. But what will come as a surprise is that the same audience is hungry for content, for projects that really mean something, and which can change lives and environments.

So Cottam isn't a designer in the purist sense. Maybe there were other worthy people in the team who transformed Kingsdale who were overlooked. But unlike Cottam they did not surface as the articulate protagonist of design as a strategic tool that can modernise schools, prisons and those public services, like health, which affect the well-being of millions. In a country that spends over half of GDP on public services and which tends to minimise the innovation and creativity that design and designers can bring, it is what Cottam's prize represents that is the real winner.

23

Defining Place

When EMBT/RMJM's Scottish parliament was named the Stirling Prize-winner at the Museum of Scotland in October 2005 two things were being recognised. One was the quality of architecture in Scotland – symbolised by the parliament – and how it has moved on since devolution. The parliament is the highest profile building in that context, however, as several international exhibitions recently curated by The Lighthouse have sought to demonstrate, it is but the centrepiece of an architectural culture that is going from strength to strength. The other thing recognised by the prize was place-making, for the parliament is not just an exquisitely wrought building it is a very significant piece of urban design. As one Stirling Prize judge expressed it, 'In its context the building manifests itself as an attempt at an organic transition between the city and the drama of the Scottish countryside surrounding it. An extremely successful landscaping makes this transition even more striking'.

With the parliament EMBT/RMJM created a place – arguably a place that will stand the test of time and outlast its competitors. And, with a huge volume of visitors that has far and away exceeded original forecasts, the parliament looks likely to become that rare thing – an unremittingly contemporary building that is both a popular and sustainable visitor destination. And, gradually, a sense of ownership is being developed. Not least, the parliament's proudest champions are its users, surely the most critical element in the poetics and politics of place-making.

How to design enduring and, indeed, popular places is the theme of this, the fourth in a series of publications related to exhibitions that jointly seek to promote Scotland's architecture and the Scottish Executive's Architecture Policy. This edition differs from its predecessors in several ways. It represents a move away from the well-tested 'yearbook' format of showcasing new buildings, by attempting to widen the debate about architecture, places and people. Of course, it features new buildings but by expanding the discussion about place aims to place them in a wider frame of reference.

As Richard Coyne, one of the contributors to this set of essays pointedly states, spaces are nowadays on trial (literally as in the case of the Scottish parliament). Non-place he contends, is the architectural equivalent of the not-proven verdict in Scots law which, in French law is *non-lieu*, and which translates as 'non-place'. This contested category of non-place is expanded to include not only the alienating and blighted but the over-branded and space over which we are denied any sense of ownership or identity, however temporary. This idea of non-place might become a test for new architecture and places and the idea of guilt or innocence offers a novel set of opposites in this context.

Craig Dykers in his opening essay adds to the discussion about our conceptions of space and place, by reminding us that the word 'shelter' invokes doing. Like the word 'place' (or indeed design) it is both noun and verb. The emphasis on *place-making* suits Dykers' idea of the verb – the doing bit – coming first, then calling the result a place; a site of human activity in other words. Dykers' word play conjures up a superb double entendre, making 'sense of place', because sense is also both subject and verb. This word play is not simply gratuitous semantics. Like the notion of guilt proven or not-proven, it makes us think about where ideas come from.

Returning to home territory, Brian Evans explores this topic further by touching on the challenges thrown up by the present interest in the New Urbanism as well as returning to the origins of identity in built form in Scotland. Evans points out in his essay that Scotland's traditional forms, like farm touns (towns) were inherently urban in their design form. They were (and this supports Dykers' contention) indisputably places – 'happening places' in common parlance – and rooted in their geographical and environmental context. This is the polar opposite of the activities of developers and volume house builders and the propensity to produce the non-places that are the focus of Coyne's contribution.

That said, identity is something that affects all of Scotland's cities and Dundee's extenuated regeneration, given the loss of almost its entire industrial past, is especially challenging. Its affluent class are lured away by the attractions of its surrounding countryside, so leaking Council Tax revenues and wealthier citizens. On the other hand, failed experiments in social housing are being replaced with new initiatives focussed on community cohesion, whilst its sunny climate has led to the exploitation of solar power. Reflecting on the tradition of Patrick Geddes who taught in the city, Simon Unwin explores the place-related consequences in the transformation of Dundee's identity, and how present housing initiatives are addressing them.

Richard Murphy's Dundee Contemporary Arts (DCA) – a previous Stirling finalist – has been closely associated with the positive re-branding of Dundee. Awarded many prizes and accolades, the much-vaunted DCA presents the ideal post-occupancy evaluation in the place v space argument. Looking at DCA in this context provides Frank Walker with the vehicle to explore how a space evolves into a place. Social relationships are as crucial as physical ones, according to Walker. Just as EMBT/RMJM's parliament building connects Edinburgh's urban edge to the Holyrood landscape, DCA joins up the River Tay to the grainy urban buzz of the city. The hinge is DCA's café-bar, a space that has become one of the most used (and loved) places in the city and unintentionally become the city's much-needed connective tissue. Importantly, it is Dundonians of all descriptions who make DCA the place that it is. An Turas, yet another former Stirling finalist, fares less well in Walker's revisitation, lacking as he perceives it, the fecund social relationships enjoyed by DCA. As a beautiful object An Turas has presence but its function in the community as a shelter is less perceptible. Existing in the ambiguous space between art and architecture, how does An Turas plead?

To be versed in the ideas propounded by Coyne and Dykers is essential if one is to interrogate the suburban brandscape of Scotland; what Mark Williamson refers to in his essay as designer Wayne Hemingway's lament about the 'Wimpification of Britain'. Volume house-builders, like their retail equivalents, are selling life-style brands to the mass consumer. The idea of designer guilt or innocence maybe has some resonance here. In a world dominated by profit margins how can you insinuate the argument about place-making? Brand is bland to paraphrase Williamson. But there are contemporary exemplars in Scotland as Williamson points out and historical precedents abound that suggest alternative, more imaginative and creative approaches.

The guilty plea could well be directed at many of so-called public art projects that have been commissioned throughout the country over the past thirty years. As Angus Farquar reflects most of these have met with complete indifference by the communities they were intended to affect. The trend for contemporary work, he contends, has not only improved the profile of public art but also allowed for a new flexibility – for briefs to respond to altering conditions. This approach opens up a new set of possibilities. The lack of permanence allows fresh perspective to emerge without the imposition of fixture. Farquar also differentiates between making art for urban and rural settings. In either context his respect for the socio/historical aspects of the site, which brings his approach closer to public design, obviates the crimes committed by many public artists. Farquar, and his organisation NVA, have created a new narrative for working in the public domain. Whether in rural or urban settings, place-making is at the centre of NVA's work. It offers an imaginative approach that is international in import and which eschews the polarisation of much of the contemporary debate about artistic and design intervention in our cities and landscapes.

The parliament debate itself was conducted in almost schizophrenic extremes and its capital location is no stranger to the Scottish Antizyzygy – Hugh MacDairmid's zig-zagging of opposites; heritage v contemporary, neo-classicism v modernism, one-way v two-way, tram v car, place v non-place. Contemporary Edinburgh is characterised by these polarities it seems, more than its European counterparts. Setting the context for a widened debate, Ricardo Marini, Edinburgh's design adviser, concludes this set of essays by delineating the debate over Edinburgh, this world heritage city whose historic core, in sharp contrast to its industrial neighbour in the West, has barely been altered over two centuries, and which is now on the cusp of massive change. The challenge it would appear, and maybe the parliament is the benchmark, is to retain Edinburgh's identity whilst facing up to the demands of twenty-first century urbanism.

In a democracy, architecture and politics share a common goal in that they are committed to improving people's living conditions. Making places should concern everyone, as architecture and urbanism operate at the interface of economics, politics and culture. This set of essays has raised a question: whose culture do buildings, spaces and landscapes serve? Who confers ownership, belonging? Architecture's public function is also meant to underpin democratic functions that underpin democratic interests. The reality is that, more often than not, economic and political motives dominate the decision-making process. Democracy presupposes and fosters equality, but capital developments sometimes generate inequality. These conflicting forces manifest themselves in designs for our social and residential environments as much as they do in commercial developments. That's why we end up with trash spaces that no one wants to live in. What this set of essays also serves to demonstrate is that there are clearly other ways of doing things that move beyond the ambiguity of not-proven.

24

Global Warning

In December while the Scottish art world was rounding on the Draft Culture Bill, bemoaning the idea of Creative Scotland and the loss of the 'arms length principal', and arguing who should take responsibility for Scotland's Creative Industries, another, potentially far more important, cultural study was emerging from Brussels. This new independent study from the European Commission underlines the changing way in which Europeans – Scots included – earn their living. Throughout Europe people are now much more likely to work in sectors such as television, fashion or other 'niche' jobs than in a factory. The sector employs nearly 6 million people, greater than the population of many EC countries, and in 2003 turned over €650 billion. What is important about this study and what makes it hugely relevant to situation in Scotland is the way in which it measures socio-economic impact and so redefines the scope of the culture sector. It moves us away from a parochial argument about the merger of the Scottish Arts Council and Scottish Screen and their ultimate control by providing a refreshingly wider European perspective. It also offers pointers for the way that Scotland might actually take a lead in the development of its cultural and creative industries.

There have been many extravagant claims in the past few years about the sector's economic value but for the first time this European study endorses what many could only previously assert, that the cultural sector is the engine of creativity, and creativity is the basis for social and economic innovation. Of course, seizing upon creativity as the economic salvation that will fight off competition from emerging economies is not new. The 2005 Cox Review commissioned by the Treasury set out creativity as the key to national prosperity as well as providing a stark warning, emphasising that all of the world's emerging economies are investing in creative capabilities. Like the European study, the Cox Review gave a crisp analysis of the situation as well as a succinct definition of creativity and innovation. Since then Cox has continued to underline the global challenges – India wants to be a global design hub and is committed to a network of academic and business centres of excellence; Singapore, Korea, Taiwan and Thailand have spent millions setting up design centres; China has opened up a staggering 400 specialists design schools; and the New Zealand prime minister is seeking to grow a cohort of design-led businesses capable of competing globally.

Unfortunately the impact of the Cox Review in Scotland, in contrast with the activity it has generated in England, seems to be minimal. In fact comparing the amount of energy and initiative generated in England around the cultural and creative industries with the almost total lack of activity in Scotland is baffling. South of the border there has been the Cox Review (and a host of follow-up activities), the Creative Economy initiative which is seeking to make the UK's (sic) Creative Industries the most competitive in the world and numerous initiatives by the energetic Regional Development Authorities working in partnership with the Design Council. In Scotland by comparison we have had the Cultural Commission, the Draft Culture Bill and Creative Scotland - lots of discussion on structure and gover-nance but precious little content. When we are asked whether Creative Scotland should have an 'economic development role for the creative industries' how should we respond? The Consultation Document defines the Creative Industries to include design, music, publishing, literature, craft, designer fashion film, computer games and TV and radio. What it does not explain fully is how these relate to the wider arts and culture fields. Far less does it expound the wider global context.

This where the new European study is useful; it defines the culture sector as 'non-industrial sectors' producing non-reproducible goods and services that are consumed on the spot – exhibitions, concerts, festivals. This is the arts field – visual and performing arts as well as heritage. In the creative sector culture becomes a 'creative' input in the production of non-cultural goods, largely through design – fashion, interior, games, and product. Thus, creativity becomes a source of innovation; this links with the Cox Review, which clearly underlines the connection between creativity, innovation and design.

All of this really matters to Scotland because in 2006 for the first time the Scottish Executive published data on Scotland's Creative Industries showing that the Gross Added Value per employee in the sector is £69,000. It is an amazing figure because £69K is twice the value of manufacturing and is catching up fast on the sector with the highest value, electronics. But despite the fantastic growth in the Creative Industries in Scotland, there are signs that they are under serious threat. In line with the rest of the UK, employment is falling due not least to increased international competition from the Far East. At the same time there is the bizarre lack of investment by our national enterprise agency. All of this sounds warning signs, not just for the Creative Economy and anyone who wants Scotland to develop world-class creative enterprises, but also for the providers of our future talent – our art schools and universities. This is the crucial aspect missing from the Culture Bill – the connection with creativity and skills.

There is a really absurd contradiction at work here and that is the effort and expense that goes into the higher education of creative people and our creative capabilities. More than 70,000 students are studying on creative courses in HE and FE in Scotland (proportionately more than the rest of the UK). This is in stark contrast to the complete lack of economic and infrastructural support that our graduates need once they enter the workforce. Here, the European study and the Cox Review converge neatly. Both want a greater emphasis on creativity and enterprise education from school through to professional levels. The recent Leitch Review of Skills could also be used in this debate. Despite it being an English document its implications, especially the need for investment in creative capabilities, cannot be avoided. Creative Scotland cannot do without the tertiary education sector, not just in terms of developing talent; it also needs its research and innovation, especially its world-class design capability. This last is the connective tissue that aggregates value in the Creative and Cultural Sector.

Against the bigger UK, European and global backdrop and the recognition that the cultural and creative sector is reinventing and redefining itself beyond the traditional and stereotypical, perhaps counter-intuitively Creative Scotland begins to make sense. Maybe the coming together of the former functions of the Scottish Arts Council, Scottish Screen with a new economic development role for the Creative Industries heralds a fresh approach. And, the closer relationship of this new body with Scottish ministers who also have responsibility for education and training holds out possibilities for more joined-up actions. If the creative capacity of Scotland's Higher Education sector could somehow be added to the mix then Scotland with its economies of scale, familial institutional relationships and cross-memberships could lead in making Europe the most competitive and dynamic knowledge-based economy in the world.

25

Designs on Making Scotland Competitive

Talk of independence and growing national confidence might well have fired the recent election but if you are Scots and work in the Creative and Cultural Industries (CCIs) you have to look to Westminster for a political lead. The CCIs have been one of the big ideas of the decade. Never before have animators, film-makers, architects and designers enjoyed such political prominence. According to Gordon Brown the sector will soon be worth 10% of the economy. But despite the high profile, if Scotland's CCIs are to move forward, providing access to finance and business support is essential. This one of the concerns of the DCMS's Creative Economy Programme, which will have an impact throughout the UK, especially in redefining the CCIs and highlighting the role of Design as the crucial link between creativity and innovation. Understanding design in Scotland means looking at the wider UK context.

One of the main drivers south of the border is the Cox Review of Creativity in Business commissioned by – who else? – Gordon Brown. Its message is that designers and business need to understand one another better. The world has moved on since Cox was published in 2005; the first person to recognise that is Cox himself. He has emphasised recently how global economies are moving even faster to build design into their business base. India's Prime Minister has launched a national plan to turn his country into a global design hub. By 2009 Singapore will have spent £160million on its national design centre. China has opened a staggering 400 specialist design schools. Helen Clark, the New Zealand Prime Minister is seeking to grow a cohort of design-led firms with the capacity to compete globally. South Korea now produces 36,000 skilled designers a year and is second only to the US, which produces 38,000. The message about design is clear – the rest of the world seems to get it; what about Scotland?

Although there has been a lot of talk about creativity and the CCIs there is a problem with definitions. Cox talks about creativity but he really means design. That is not legerdemain; it is just how you get around the politics of creativity. Recent research by NESTA has suggested a different four-part structure: Creative Service Providers – advertising, architecture or design consultancies; Creative Content Producers – games, film production companies or fashion designers; Creative Experience Providers – festival promoters, dance companies; Creative Originals Producers – craft-makers, visual artists. This is reinforced by the Creative Economy Programme, which has structured the creative sector into three elements: Production, Services and Arts and Crafts. More recent research commissioned by the EC has shown that culture drives economic and social development as well as innovation and cohesion. Innovation is important because NESTA has underlined very recently how the current metrics do not reflect the true level of innovation in the UK. In other words, why do we appear to have an innovation gap when design and the creative industries are growing at exponential levels? The national, European and international context is changing; what about Scotland?

Scotland has no dedicated support for design. There is no longer a Design Council presence or a national design policy. Scottish Enterprise long ago gave up on design and the Creative Industries. Emerging designers can access the services of Business Gateway, the Cultural Enterprise Office or other generic support. But is that really enough to create the design-led businesses that will compete globally as demanded by Cox? The findings of the Creative Economy Programme apply as much to Scotland as they do to the rest of the UK: the central issue is not finance but access and use; the need for dedicated business development support; the lack of skills; and the need for more commercially focussed networks. This is not news. Creative and Cultural Skills in Scotland has identified a sector dominated by micro businesses unable to invest in training, with graduates lacking business and entrepreneurial skills.

Those needs have to be explored further. Both design users and designers lack the skills demanded by the fast changing global environment. SMEs lack the skills to manage design as a core business discipline. The design industry's fragmented 'cottage industry' structure undermines its influence across business and education. Science and technology in Scotland fails to integrate design in the commercialisation of new ideas. The current HE model of Knowledge Transfer does not recognise design's business models and value chains. Business leaders do not know how to exploit design. The Scottish Executive does not lead with design in public procurement. Market for sustainably designed products and services is lacking. Designers are ill equipped to guide clients on technical sustainability issues or new service design approaches.

We need the expertise of the Design Council here in Scotland. We need to successfully integrate design, business and entrepreneurship courses. At The Robert Gordon University, Gray's School of Art has successfully developed industry-led design courses that integrate business and entrepreneurship and jointly developed CCI courses with the Aberdeen Business School. Instead of an extension of Knowledge Transfer schemes we need a new conceptualisation that recognises the way design performs in the real world – its creative interactions, personal engagement and networks. We need to raise awareness of the competitive opportunities presented by sustainable design. We need to market design and design strategy to the public and the private sector. Can we influence the new government in Scotland to be the 'best small design nation'?

Scotland produces world-class designers but that will not

matter unless post election we recognise that a world-leading economy needs a high quality design sector. That requires intervention. The Koreans, Taiwanese, Singaporeans and Chinese get it. It is about time we did.

26

The Creative Class in Scotland

Scotland's new SNP administration may have given up its predecessor's aspiration to be the 'best small country in the world' but the Westminster government still wants the UK to be the world's creative hub.

What many politicians and civil servants do not seem to get is the irritation that is felt by the creative industries community not only at the seemingly endless consultations and half-hearted interventions, but also the confusion caused by the woolliness of the terms that are bandied about. Part of the problem is that the sector is hard to understand.

Certainly, creativity is at its core, but explaining what the connection is between people working in areas as diverse as advertising, fashion, music, film, architecture, or design is difficult and therefore difficult to support. What is also poorly understood in Scotland, though not in many other places, is what links these disparate activities, namely design. Design is the connective tissue, the golden thread. That is why new design centres and design support agencies are springing up all over the world. Design is the key ingredient in developing, packaging and presenting products and services. A world without design would be a world with no iPods, no Dyson cleaners, no Shrek, no mountain bikes – the list is endless.

A consensus is emerging that the challenge for policy-makers is to reflect the highly distributed, self-organising, post-industrial ecology of the creative industries themselves. They represent a new way of living and working; they constitute a 'creative class'. It is not sufficient for support to be 'delivered' via an old industrial model, or polyglot organisation unable to work out whether its remit should be economic or cultural, subsidy or investment.

Crucial to this new policy awareness is the understanding that we are living in an age of mass creativity. More and more consumers are becoming producers. This is especially true among young people, who understand culture as something they remake to create their own meanings and identities. This production of meaning is now the primary industry in post-industrial economies. Research by bodies such as investment group NESTA indicate that the creative industries need dedicated, sector specific solutions and support to encourage this. Studies by Demos shows that people in the creative industries have work and employment patterns that change quickly to meet market opportunities. They cannot be supported by static university courses, generic business advice and regulatory bodies. But the apparent absence of planning and the application of traditional business skills puts off investors.

The SNP administration could seek to address these problems. Their 'Big Conversation' could generate a new narrative appropriate to the age of mass creativity. The emphasis is on tool-kits instead of policy directives, self-help over dependency, networks as opposed to agencies, micro-finance not public subsidy, brokerage as an alternative to managerialism, distributed partnerships replacing a centralist body. In Scotland we should see the proliferation of creativity as nothing less than the evolution of democracy.

27

Gray's Anatomy: Why Ceramics Education in Scotland Hasn't Quite Died

This article questions the demise of crafts within Art and Design (as the subject as it is known in Higher Education [HE]), especially given the recent elevation of the importance of craft by commentators such as Sennett who, in his book *The Craftsman* (2008), has extended the definition of craft, saying that it can be seen in the scientific laboratory as well as the studios of potters or jewellers; for him it means doing a job well for its own sake. Sennett also believes craftsmanship is a basic human impulse as it involves contact with material – a satisfying physical relationship that is a fundamental human need. As such, Sennett believes craft is as important in modern society as it ever was. Privileging crafts in this way also parallels the rise of slow movements in time, travel, food and work in response to the ever-increasing demand for acceleration. Sennett estimates that it takes 10,000 hours to become a craftsman, the same length of time celebrated *Tipping Point* author Malcolm Gladwell believes it takes to develop expert competence, which is arguably another definition of craft.

Despite this, many specialist craft degree courses – for example ceramics and glass – have disappeared, and many are under threat (and this must be confusing for those entering Art and Design courses). There are several reasons for this. One is the prevailing philosophy in Art & Design at HE level that the need for high level craft skills has been displaced by new technologies. However, if Sennett is to be believed, digital technology, which is ever changing and immediate, far from eliminating the crafts, has thrown up the need for us to connect to the material world. Another is the increasingly conceptual nature of fine art coupled with a trend in design towards becoming a strategic tool to enhance business performance, and a mistaken perception that the crafts, because of their concern for the material, are less capable of expressing ideas. This is contradicted by eminent critic and director of the Design Museum, Deyan Sudjic, in his recent book *The Language of Things* (2008). Sudjic contends that objects are how we define ourselves, to signal who we are, whether jewellery, furniture or clothing. It is designers and craftsmen who shape those objects and customise the messages they carry. He also believes, like Sennett, that crafts are essential to building aircraft, spaceships, and the Formula One car industry.

The contemporary role of crafts in expressing ideas connects with new concepts like the design/artist, forcing both a rethink of the intermediate role of crafts and the strengthening of its relationship to both art and design. Self-styled design artist Geoff Mann believes that the role of craft has 'mutated through its own fluidity'. According to him, the cross-pollination of art, craft and design has stimulated a new hybrid practice and has created practitioners who are astute generalists. If this is so, then the use of craft in aggregating value to create a new-found flexibility demands to be recognised as an important development for the creative industries. Likewise, Simon Ward is a ceramicist who works with traditional techniques like slip-casting, using materials like porcelain to create pieces for both domestic and outdoor contexts. But his work is also about ideas. In one of his outdoor pieces for a Sculpture trail – a porcelain casting of a tree trunk – Ward incorporated video, passing a camera through the moulds to give the viewer a sense of what it would be like to be inside a tree. Really, crafts, design and art should be seen as a continuum, where mutual influences and collaborations have led to a much more nuanced situation. Jeweller Wendy Ramshaw is an example of this; her work moves effortlessly from jewellery to site-specific and architectural installations with commissions in steel, glass and gold leaf. Other terms like non-industrial design and design-led crafts are other facets of this interaction, where crafts provide designers with opportunities for individual expression as well as an excellent way of telling stories and visualising ideas, while design offers its continuous quest for creativity and economies of scale, as well as its social ambitions. Matched to this trend, the irreversible process of 'eco' design enhances the relevance of a society embracing a real and much-needed environmental consciousness impacting our quality of life. In this, Crafts' traditional values such as revival, nostalgia, slowness, patience, individualisation, manual skills and authenticity offer a new narrative.

Crafts, inseparable from design, and now linked to art, play a crucial role in the UK's Creative and Cultural Industries. Craftsmanship is the new black (or green). It can be the connective tissue between art and design as well as a creative medium and a driver of innovation. And, its focus on skills – on making – renders its graduates and practitioners valuable in the post-global economic crisis. Further evidence of this is provided by a recent study by NESTA. This research focussed on how fine arts graduates contribute to innovation both within the arts and the wider economy. Given the similarities in their art school education, the findings could apply to crafts, as much as fine arts graduates. The research found that these graduates possess the attitudes and skills that are conducive to innovation and that they also see themselves as brokers across disciplines. Central to the findings were experimentation and openness to new ideas, skills that are also prized in the crafts, and which are valuable in the creative economy. It can be seen, therefore, that those contemplating a career in the crafts or already working in the field are entering or operate in an area that has much to offer economically, socially and culturally. Not least, there is the personal satisfaction of engagement with the material world that the crafts can offer. The question remains whether these qualities are appreciated within HE?

Clearly, because of changes in society, especially attempts to relieve the ills of contemporary capitalism, the crafts with their emphasis on high levels of dedicated skill, are now seen as having much to offer. What is extremely important in the crafts is that they are democratic – skill in any area can be improved. There is no demarcation between the gifted elite and the simply competent. Whether this external recognition is similarly appreciated by the Art and Design HE sector is debatable given its prioritisation of digital technology over slowly developing craft skills and mass education over intensive tutor/student contact; from electronic exchanges to personal relationships.

To regenerate crafts in HE art and design a number of things are necessary so that it reflects its newfound economic, social and cultural status. HE art and Design needs to recognise:

- the relevance of craftsmanship as antidote to the dehumanising aspects of the accelerated speed of our globalised society
- the basic human need to connect with the material world, which crafts can provide
- the transferability of crafts skills across disciplines and contexts
- the ability of crafts to connect disciples and link art and design, therefore aggregating value
- the ability of crafts to express ideas and concepts and communicate identity and narratives
- the convergence of crafts, art and design and the ability of those educated in the crafts to move between these areas
- the role of crafts in bridging creativity and innovation and the value of experimentation and openness to ideas to the creative economy

28

Sun, Sex and TEA

Relax: there is little danger that our traditional beverage has supplanted Sangria, the drink beloved by British tourists to Spain. TEA – Tenerife Espacio de les Artes, designed by Swiss architects Herzog & De Meuron, which opened last November, is a stunning contemporary art institute, a photography centre and a public library in Santa Cruz, Tenerife's capital. The island has a population of only 800,000 and Tenerife just over 200,000. As a city like Aberdeen, which is comparable in size to Santa Cruz, struggles to launch a contemporary art centre, what is astonishing about TEA is that this is merely the latest in a succession of exceptional buildings that have gone up recently in Tenerife. What's also remarkable in a place known more for the rash of kitsch holiday accommodation that proliferates across Tenerife's volcanic hillsides than high-quality architecture, is that TEA is no one-off. And, what's happening in the Canaries at the very edge of the EU has lots of lessons for Scotland.

TEA is one of three projects by Herzog & De Meuron in Santa Cruz. The Swiss firm completed the remodelling of the Plaza of Spain in the summer of 2007 and is currently working on transforming the city's port into a residential and recreational area. TEA joins Calatrava's wave-like Auditorium and the moat-like sports stadium by local practice AMP architects, adding to Tenerife's architectural reputation. Comparable Scottish and UK cities would be challenged to list one world-class contemporary building, never mind a catalogue full.

Further down the coast in Adeje is the brutalist-designed Magma Arts and Congress Center also by AMP, opened in 2006. In this centre irregular, bush-hammered concrete forms gather into a rugged sculptural group under an airy white roof, evoking

Le Corbusier's neoprimitive architecture at Chandigarh, but is entirely sympathetic with Tenerife's volcanic geology and the conversion of molten lava into stone in the surrounding landscape.

Herzog and De Meuron also respect the context of Tenerife whilst exploiting the physical and material challenges offered to them. TEA is a low-slung, shadow-like structure that spills out over the ground just where Santa Cruz's old and new elements meet, covering an area of over 20,000 sq m. The building's exteriors are finished in pumice-grey concrete, pierced by small bubble-like glass-filled openings in random patterns. It is sited along a steep gorge, the Barranco de Santos, on the western edge of the historic centre. They have created a public footpath that descends diagonally through the building from the top of the site to the banks of the Barranco. In the middle the path broadens to become a triangular-shaped entry plaza. Part-covered, this plaza is enlivened by the café, and overlooks the transparent space of the library's main reading room through continuous glass walls. The upper level houses top-lit galleries for the permanent collection, while the lower level contains temporary exhibition spaces and the photography galleries. The two floors are connected to the entry lobby by a sweeping spiral stair. An elongated triangular geometry of folded planes extends throughout the building, including a number of patios scattered among interior spaces. Natural light inside and shady spaces outside are particular features of how interior and exterior elements interconnect.

It would be difficult to put Scotland on a par with Spain in terms of using architecture to communicate a newfound identity, EMBT/RMJM's Scottish Parliament building notwithstanding. However, the Canaries, with a small population and also located at the periphery of the EU, do make a useful comparison. Tenerife is an exemplar of using architecture to express local identity whilst aspiring to being world class. Importantly, this is being achieved with a combination of home-grown and international talent and an obvious respect for geography and heritage. In a stringent economic climate the Canaries are diversifying their economy to attract the global market in events and conferencing by creating world-class public buildings with the best architects. In this country as we contemplate a programme of infrastructural projects to lessen the effects of the global financial crisis, it may be instructional to observe the architectural lesson of Tenerife and the Canaries as they blow apart the stereotype of sun and sangria.

29

Aberdeen's City Square Project Represents a Loss of Democracy

Like many UK cities Aberdeen has suffered its fair share of post-war architectural travesties including some grotesque dislocations of scale. Recent developments, including the proposal to create a vast city centre square by decking over Union Terrace Gardens are little different. Promoted by entrepreneur Sir Ian Wood and backed by the local economic forum, this new civic space would create a 5-6 acre space comparable to Moscow's Red Square or Glasgow's George Square. Those squares relate to large or dense urban populations. In comparison, Aberdeen and its hinterland has a population of only 400,000. Could that number animate a space the size of Red Square? Why would you want to anyway?

Post Copenhagen, any proposal to bury a historical green space in the centre of a city under thousands of tons of environmentally toxic concrete has to be subjected to the utmost scrutiny. But it is not only the obliteration of an important piece of natural heritage that is at stake. Also in danger is Aberdeen's chance to have a rare piece of contemporary architecture. Brisac Gonzales' scheme for a new arts centre with planning permission and most of its funding in place, is situated on three stepped terraces within the Gardens and is exemplary in several ways. It will create a relationship between building and garden, art and nature, similar to Denmark's world-famous Louisiana Art Gallery. Equally unique, it will be entered via the roof, an expansive urban space with a host of different activities – market, bookstalls, exhibitions and cafe, attracting visitors, enriching urban life and serving as living signage for what will be a highly inclusive arts centre. Most important for Aberdeen and for

Scotland, the new centre may be one of the best contemporary public buildings of the decade and re-affirm the city as a place of ideas, enterprise and culture. Unfortunately, the Wood scheme obviates the Brisac Gonzales design.

Aberdeen makes a stark contrast with its neighbour Dundee which, because of the regenerative impact of Dundee Contemporary Arts, can contemplate hosting a satellite of the V&A and entertain designs by the likes of Frank Gehry. The quality of the Brisac Gonzales building, its likely regenerative effect and all the research on creative cities seems lost on the Wood's scheme's promoters. Given the controversy, huge expense, unsustainability, and the cost of the PR juggernaut promoting this proposal, you would have thought that the most extensive civic debate was merited. Consultation in this context has amounted only to the 'square's' supporters offering a single choice, the complete decking over of the gardens as a given but with some additions.

This one-sidedness runs counter to best practice in consultation in the public realm and against the latest Scottish Government planning advice calling for effective community engagement to ensure that: 'people are made aware of proposals that affect them as early in the process as is possible, that they have the facts to allow them to make a contribution, that they have had the opportunity to engage and that having made their views known, they get clearer explanations of how and why decisions were made'. There are lessons here for other UK cities and there is more at stake than the loss of either a green space or the chance of having a world-class building. Democracy itself may be the loser.

30

The Future is Digital?

The aim of this year's NEON conference – collaborating across gaming, visual communication, entertainment and the arts and increasing our digital knowledge is not just crucial for the future of the digital sector and creative industries generally, but absolutely important for the future of our cities as well. In these dire economic times Creative and Cultural Industries are the future lifeblood of our cities – it is just that not enough people recognise it. NEON has a great programme with lots of really interesting people talking about digital arts who know much more about the sector than I do. So, to be useful, I thought I would stick to talking what I know about, which is digital developments as part of the creative industries especially in the context of cities and pick out some more interesting collaborations, identify some trends like 'ecotainmant' and touch on real-world issues like 'The Big Society'.

Eggs and Headless Chickens

I have to confess that I am no futurologist. My experience of futurology, certainly in the Dundee context, is limited to the prophesies of Elspet Renkyne, the red-haired witch burnt to the stake in the market place in seventeenth century Dundee in William Blain's book *Witches Blood*. If you remember, she prophesied that the power was in her blood and would be too powerful for a small town like Dundee. According to Elspet, the blood would go and go and go many times and return and return many times and in it's returning the blood would sometimes bring back what's needed. What you have keep in mind is that the scene-setter to Elspet's marketplace prophesies was the amazing sight of a headless chicken laying an egg in the city centre. It is an image I cannot dismiss when people talk about great visions for a city.

Where is the Future?

If the future is digital where can we go to see it? City visions? The announcement last week of Kenga Kuma's winning design for the V&A on Tayside coincided with my return from Shanghai – and if you believe the pundits China is the future. Primarily, I went there to see the Shanghai Expo, which was amazing in scale and spectacle and indicative of what is happening in China more generally. But I also went to see the Shanghai Urban Planning Exhibition Centre. Not the sexiest of names for what is the most popular visitor attraction in Shanghai with literally hundreds of thousands of people – the majority working class Chinese as far as I could see – pouring through the doors. The attraction is a gigantic model of Shanghai showing how the city is going to develop over the next few years. How it comes alive is through numerous, high quality interactives, which invite people to participate and comment on the planning decisions that are going to affect their lives in every possible way. On the one hand this confounds your preconceptions of a totalitarian state, but on the other it is a large-scale demonstration of helping citizens engage with the key challenges of our time – urban design, sustainability, climate change, health, transport – all using digital technology. If look at it in another way, as well as facilitating citizen participation, a mass audience for interactive technology and digital media is also being grown. Interestingly, most of the interactives – the best I've seen anywhere – were powered by games engines, used the latest motion graphics and 3D, and as far I could gather, were all created by Chinese designers.

The point is that here is a communist city regime with a population of 20 million harnessing the power of digital technology to address real-world issues in a way that we, in supposedly democratic Scotland with a population of only 5 million, are not. If you think about the Trump debacle in Aberdeenshire, the outcry about filling in Union Terrace Gardens in Aberdeen, the argument about Edinburgh's greenbelt or indeed the issues around Kenga Kuma's V&A building, where are the opportunities for Scotland's citizens to engage in the debate facilitated by the latest digital technology in a compelling way and why is Government not exploiting that market? By the way, the Chinese Premier no less said recently that he wants to move from 'Made in China' to 'Designed in China'. China already accounts for more than 80 per cent of the global supply of digital cameras and portable DVD players. Chinese technological progress in mobile entertainment and communications is driving production and R&D at an incredible rate. And, despite the fact that they occasionally chuck them in prison, China's future depends upon its artists and creatives. But the real future will be in how the regime manages its growing affluence and demands for greater democracy, and the role digital democracy will play. Whether we like it or not because of globalisation our future is bound up with that of China. My feeling is that it will continue to confound our expectations.

Is Ecotainment the Future?

It is all very well to tackle invasions of zombies and aliens, gang violence in New York or even engage in *Modern Warfare*, but can computer games address other challenges? Recently, there has been a flowering of issue-led gaming with the launch of the British designed *Fate of the World* in which players are at the helm of a future World Trade Organisation-type environmental body tasked with saving the world by cutting carbon emissions. *Fate of the World*, which follows on from earlier 'ecotainment' games like *World Without Oil*, is being hailed by gaming experts as a break-through for social change titles and by climate campaigners as a way of reaching new audiences. It may be why, as gaming expert Tom Chatfield claims in his book of the same name, *Games are the*

21st Century's Most Serious Business. And, of course, in the next few years because of developments in 3D display and motion control and things like Xbox Kinect, any firm concept of what constitutes a computer game will require radical revision.

But for me what the Shanghai Urban Planning Centre, Fate of the World and other issue-led games from health to human rights, show, as Bill Mitchell said, is that the future is already here, it is just that it is not very evenly distributed. That's why we need more co-creation and more co-design, and that means a new way of thinking. In other words, as well as continuing to develop the entertainment market or the new trend for 'ecotainment' and websites sites like *carbonrally* and *earthlab*, how can we get the digital media sector onto the well-being agenda because that is a huge growth area and a top political priority. It seems to me, that as well as keeping an eye on China and Asia, this is a clear direction for us to go in.

Digital Democracy

To take this a little further. The idea that 'content is king' has been a regularly repeated mantra in the internet revolution. Now we are moving into a digital future where it is not simply the content that is king but the context and way that content is experienced. As content becomes available across multiple platforms the challenge for content creators will be to understand what the user experience is like across these multiple platforms. The better the experience, the more likely people are to consume more and pay more. This is where the creative industries come in by helping to define and design this experience, putting it at the heart of all the activities that seek to enhance not just consumption, but what Charles Leadbeater calls prosumption.

As content converges across platforms, and platforms themselves converge, creative businesses are facing the challenge of their boundaries blurring and business models altering.

Business will increasingly need to collaborate to create whole new content experiences. Increasingly, consumers (or prosumers) want to be the authors of their own narratives. Therefore, TV production companies and games companies have an even greater opportunity to work together to extend the reach of their products so a TV programme becomes a computer game. This meets the increasing consumer demand to interact with content in different ways on their own terms and, at a time of their choosing, replacing the traditional linear delivery model of TV.

I have a question for you: How might the creative and cultural industries mobilise to push out new meanings and experiences? This is I think where festivals like NEON have a role. For example, for the past decade most of the debate about creative and cultural industries has focussed on audience development and has tended to be a marketing-led, top-down model. That is why I think the discussion about prosuming and emerging models of co-design is so intriguing. They point the way to a user-generated state. A business or arts organization that treats people simply as consumers or just an audience if you like – even well treated ones – will miss the point about the successful new organisational models emerging from Web 2.0. or Film 2.0.

Privacy

The other big issue about the future that is already here, and one that we cannot escape, concerns privacy. Everyday web users leave a trail of data about themselves as they surf the net. This free data about all aspects of people's lives is harvested by some organisations to help drive their business offering. However, as the issue of privacy becomes increasingly important, people will recognise the value of the data they give away and expect to trade it for content that has real value to them. This trade-off is likely to involve trusted third parties having permission to access rich data such as user profiles, historical activity and buying habits. The idea of trading privacy for content is a massive shift from the current thinking that says content is either free or paid for. It will require a high degree of transparency but opens the door for whole new business opportunities for creative companies.

Filmocracy

But going back to Web 2.0 and Film 2.0. As video games become more like movies and movies increasingly use 3D virtual environments as the backdrop to their productions, the other trend is that innovative film-making of all kinds is growing as digitization democratizes making movies by reducing cost. So, just to give one example, you get Web 2.0 sites like *IndieGoGo.com* promising 'filmocracy' by providing an open platform for film-makers to pitch their projects. Like the crowd funding of the Obama presidential campaign, *IndieGoGo.com* promotes the idea of many investors providing small amounts of money. You don't need to be a Dundonian witch to work that out that the world of games, gaming and the visual entertainment industry generally, is only going to get more and more interesting. . Nor is there any reason why creatives in Scotland cannot be part of that innovation. We certainly don't lack talent. But we do lack tax breaks and other financial incentives. But it is not just tax breaks we need. We need much more robust policies that truly understand and join up what the digital and creative industries and their role in contemporary economies is about. Take manufacturing, which politicians believe is central our economic recovery. If you take an extreme example like the car industry and its industrial-age problems, how could you transform its fortunes?

Mass Collaboration

This is no issue-led computer game. In the US Local Motors is a radical new form of car company led by an ex-marine called Jay Rogers. He doesn't employ a design team and he doesn't do any in-house R&D. He has an on-line community of almost 5,000 designers from 120 countries, who collectively design next-generation cars. He doesn't have a conventional supply chain, he sources parts from existing manufacturers and suppliers. Nor does he have a huge factory, rather a network of 35 micro factories each employing local workers. Likewise there are no dealerships; cars are sold directly from the microfactories. It is a decentralized mass collaboration model.

I am not suggesting that you could resuscitate a long-dead UK or even deader Scottish car industry. I am quite simply using it as an example of what Don Tapscott now calls 'macrowikinomics', or collaborative innovation enabled by the web. The economic extension of Twitter, Facebook and Wikipedia. It also allows me to make another point which is that you may see a lot of future innovation coming from novel collaborations; digital designers working with product engineers or architecture practices uncoupling themselves from the construction industry to offer wider digital services and products to clients. The sad thing is when you read government policies like 'Digital Britain' I don't think politicians get the social, economic and cultural revolution that's happening with digitization.

One of our problems looking to the future is that very few creative firms or organisations have the critical mass of in-house skills and market knowledge fully to exploit market opportunities or generate creativity through in-house teams of sufficient diversity. They need to be able to network with others to fill gaps in their knowledge and skill sets. There is a strong case for greater brokerage, especially through the web, to enable this to happen to exploit market opportunities. It should also focus on the public sector – to the wider well-being agenda. As well as user-generated content spawning social networking sites and mass computer games like the *World of Warcraft* it also extends to the development of Scottish-designed sites like MyPolice, which offers a facility for people to communicate confidentially with the police, and in the health service the ALISS Engine that connects service designers with patients and their health needs.

A Really Big (Digital) Society

This innovation shift to co-creation, co-design and co-production is growing and influencing public service delivery. Prosuming in the public sector if you like. To put it another way, Government policy to deliver citizen-centred public services at greater value for money needs policy-makers and commissioners to learn how to harness user-centred creativity amongst other things, to achieve innovation. The Big Society (and I tread carefully here) requires a new approach, and down South organisations like the Design Council, NESTA and others like ACE are refocusing their efforts to help bring about the change needed to deliver this. Regardless what we may think about the Big Society, in the context of our current economic state delivering better, cheaper public services is an inescapable concern and, I would contend, a major opportunity for Creative Industries and the digital sector. As yet I don't hear much discussion about it despite the size of our public sector here in Scotland.

Summary

Forecasting, as the red-haired witch found out, is not risk-free. I have tried to highlight some directions. Sure, I didn't mention affordable broadband access although that's central to much of what I've been talking about. Nor did I really get into the issues in the Digital Britain or indeed Digital Inspiration – the Strategy for Scotland's Digital Media Industry. Never mentioned education and we could spend years discussing that topic. Equally I didn't highlight enough of the innovation in Dundee and around but you know about all that already.

But I did mention: China-proofing, mass collaboration – the idea of the world as your R&D department, issue-led gaming, digital media and tackling real-word problems, embracing the well-being agenda and using creativity and imagination to improve public services, and not least the need for more robust policies that reflect the reality of the culture shifts that are happening locally and globally. And I did say that NEON was fantastic? So, finally, is digital the blood? Of course it is and still is, very definitely, in Dundee.

31

Joined-Up Creativity: Creative Industries and Scotland's Urban and Rural Creative Economy

Introduction

When NVA transformed the dramatic natural land formation of The Old Man of Storr in Trotternish on the Isle of Skye through illumination and sound throughout the months of August and September in 2005 they created an intense and personal experience. For 42 nights this award winning installation 'The Storr: Unfolding Landscape' brought an audience of 6500 people, equipped with headlamps, guides and walking sticks, on a strenuous walk to witness one of Europe's most dramatic and inspiring landscapes at midnight. The massed pinnacles and buttresses were illuminated while powerful soundscapes drifted down from the ridges above. As well as its cultural impact and economic impact on tourism, NVA, short for Nacionale Vitae Activa, demonstrates several key things about the creative rural economy. First is that remoteness is no barrier to mounting significant creative projects. Second it is also quite literally a model of the experience economy in which, 'work is theatre and every business a stage' (Pine and Gilmour, 1999). Third, it is an example of the project economy (Lash, 2011); in the case of NVA a core team of six people is variously expanded to suit the needs of individual projects by utilising the services of numerous freelancers, for example: lighting designers, musicians, sound engineers, film-makers and web designers. Fourth, at its core is a creative entrepreneur, Angus Farquar, who, as well as creativity, possesses the leadership expertise and skills to develop and deliver such projects; in other words, to sell the project to investors and external stakeholders, as well promote and market the experience. Fifth, there is a spillover effect on the tourism sector. Sixth, it is a potent form of branding. Crucially, the project is located within the Creative Rural Economy and not an urban context as is usually the case with CCIs.

Definitions

In a number of ways the Storr project represents the contemporary Creative Economy at whose heart are the CCIs that lie at the crossroads of culture, business and technology. What unifies these activities is the fact that they all trade with creative assets in one form or another. The notion of Creative Industries derived from the UK Government's Department for Culture, Media and Sport (DCMS) mapping exercise and definition (1998), which is: 'Those industries which have their origin in individual creativity, skill and talent and which have a potential for wealth and job creation through the generation and exploitation of intellectual property.' There are thirteen sub-sectors defined by the DCMS and these are: advertising, architecture, the art and antiques market, crafts, design, designer fashion, film and video, interactive leisure software, music, the performing arts, publishing, software and computer games, and television and radio. The term Cultural Industries is also used by some agencies, though this term relates to a more specific range of industries and can be regarded as a subset of the creative industries. In the UK the hybrid term, Creative and Cultural Industries is often used, for instance, by Creative and Cultural Skills, which is one of the UK's Learning Skills Councils (LSCs) and whose footprint includes: craft, design, cultural heritage, music, literature and performing and visual arts.

In this sense, Flew and Cunningham (2010) have described what they term 'the struggle for definitional coherence' and underline challenges to the early list-based approach and the growing consensus around what should be core to the definition of the Creative Industries. For example, the UK's National

Endowment for Science Technology and the Arts (NESTA 2006), has produced what it terms a 'refined' model for the Creative Industries that includes:

- creative experience providers – live theatre, opera or multi-media performers;
- creative content producers – film and TV companies, computer and video games studios, fashion houses;
- creative service providers – architecture practices, advertising agencies, design consultancies;
- creative originals producers – visual artists, crafts people.

NESTA maintains that this model provides for better targeting of economic growth as it separates out those who create Intellectual Property (IP). However, this illuminates another debate in a sector dominated by micro-businesses, namely, what constitutes growth? In the context of the Creative Rural economy with its geographic and demographic constraints, this is particularly contentious.

International Comparison

In terms of the global interpretation of Creative Industries, Canada and the province of Ontario offer an interesting comparison to Scotland and the UK. It is especially interesting because on the one hand it draws upon Florida's widely disseminated work on the Creative Class whilst on the other focussing on the capabilities that further creativity. Thus, Ontario has adopted a concept of the Creative Economy that considers the economy in accordance with the work people do to encompass 'creative occupations', thus adding scientists and technologists to designers and artists. Nonetheless, in Canada, whilst the Creative Economy is seen as pervasive, it is identified as being concentrated in a number of businesses that are categorised as Creative Industries. So, the Ontario definition of the Creative

Industries is similar to that of the DCMS (with the exception of Business Consulting, Engineering, Marketing and Public Relations) ostensibly making a comparison possible. Importantly, like Scotland, Ontario is seeking to build geographic advantage by harnessing the creative potential of its citizens.

In that sense, based on Florida identification of three sets of skills that 'creative workers' draw upon, namely; analytical skills, social intelligence skills and physical skills, Ontario-based economic development agencies have refined these into a set of analytical and social intelligence skills. Analytical thinking skills are related to art directors and engineers, for example, whilst social intelligence skills are linked to occupations that focus upon the management of people such as film directors and marketing managers. As Florida admits, while these skills are important components of creativity-oriented occupations, all occupations have a requirement for these skills. However, according to their research, the higher an occupation is on the analytical index, the more it pays, thus, allowing an analysis to be made in terms of the perceived financial value of creative skills across Canadian provinces or US states and by extension, Scotland and the UK. For critics of Creative Industries the Canadian approach might be evidence of the empirical weakness of the theoretical analyses it propagates, although such critiques are more often based on a weakening of the case for the arts as opposed to economic arguments. For others it is evidence of Florida's prescient analysis of the need to focus on the talent deficit and the fact that advanced nations have been living beyond their capacity to generate talent and have been borrowing to fuel growth and prosperity.

A further increment in terms of helping to contour the sector and its economy comes from a 2006 European Commission study. Where this is useful is in defining the culture sector as 'non-industrial', producing non-reproducible goods and services that are consumed on the spot – exhibitions, concerts, and festivals.

This is the arts field – visual and performing arts – as well as heritage. In the creative sector culture becomes a 'creative' input in the production of non-cultural goods, largely through design – fashion, interior, games, and product. Thus, creativity becomes a source of innovation. This links with the influential Cox Review prepared for HM Treasury, which clearly underlines the connection between creativity, innovation and design. A succession of European strategy documents have since attempted to underpin the role of the sector from unlocking their wider economic and social potential to the Amsterdam Declaration and the establishment of a European Creative Industries Alliance and the European Innovation Union. Thus, there is a sense, at the European level at least, of concerted action on Creative Industries.

Creative Scotland

Likewise, the Scottish Government has identified Creative Industries as a key priority area and established a Scottish Creative Industries Partnership (SCIP) chaired by Creative Scotland whose recently published Corporate Plan outlines the strategic role of SCIP, especially the national coordination of the various stakeholders. Scotland is probably unique in seeking to integrate the breadth of the Creative and Cultural industries in terms of policy and delivery. Creative Scotland appears to regard definitions as at least problematic; the agency's Corporate Plan talks of investing in the 'Cultural Economy' and simultaneously promoting social objectives and the responsibility to stimulate growth in the 'economy of culture and the creative industries', the latter through SCIP. In this respect Scotland is nevertheless in line with contemporary European strategy in recognizing the key drivers, namely: the need to put the right enablers in place, increasing the capacity to experiment; using local and regional development as a global launch pad; and moving towards a creative economy by catalyzing the spill-over effects of CCIs on a wide range of economic and social contexts.

A review of the recent literature for the Scottish Government has highlighted the importance of formulating a definition of the creative sector that is relevant to the context in which it is to be applied and which enables analysis to consider what is of interest to a particular policy setting. To this end, research suggests that approaches based on the wider concept of the Creative Economy (which includes the Creative Industries) may be able to overcome some of the perceived limitations. Contemporary with this review, the Scotland's Creative Industries Partnership Report and a Scottish Government Key Sector Report were published; signposting the way for the establishment of Creative Scotland in 2010.

In close succession, again for the first time, a Creative Sector Skills Action Plan, instigated by SCIP was prepared. It brought together Scotland's main public sector organisations to contribute their expertise, and advise on future opportunities for strengthening Scotland's creative industries. The purpose of this plan was to provide an industry-informed framework against which better support for more targeted skills and learning in Scotland's creative sector could be prioritised. This will be achieved by: fostering a step-change in the way in which learning and skills for Scotland's creative employers and practitioners are supported; clarifying routes to funding skills and learning that satisfy the needs of the sector; and supporting extreme collaboration across all partners and stakeholders. The role of Scotland's universities – the primary source of talent for the creative economy – has also been highlighted. Amongst its key findings are that employability and entrepreneurship are growing areas of focus for higher education and universities can be an important provider of continuing professional development for the creative industries as well as the need for greater collaboration between universities and skills and training providers.

Against that background the detailed targets and impacts of

Creative Scotland's plan attempt to enunciate national outcomes with partnership as a high priority driver in order to promote 'the unique contribution that different places, local authority areas and sub-regions play in a Creative Scotland'. Therefore, in addition to promulgating a holistic approach to creativity and culture, national policy is also committed to developing Scotland's creative urban and rural economies as well as the necessary underpinning education and training. Hence the need for a progressive evaluation that encompasses city, region, and place and the creative projects and people which animate them.

Creative City: Glasgow

Glasgow's post-industrial transformation has been well documented over two decades. In what became a global phenomenon, the transformation of cities by design and cultural regeneration, Glasgow, through its reign in 1990 as European Culture Capital, used creativity and design to define a decade. Glasgow has been a model, with its momentum-building techniques copied elsewhere. The place marketing that started with the Glasgow's 'Miles Better' campaign and was the multiplier effect in City of Culture carried through to the 1996 and 1999 city design festivals. One of the most important staging posts for Glasgow as Creative City was its reign on the eve of the Millennium as UK City of Architecture and Design. In that sense, innovation linked to the creative economy was boosted with the Lighthouse – the £12.5 million conversion of Charles Rennie Mackintosh's former *Glasgow Herald* building.

That investment has continued with the development the BBC by English architect David Chipperfield, which is also home to many 'indies' and the new Riverside Museum designed by Zaha Hadid; Trongate 103 which houses numerous cultural enterprises; Film City, again a conversion of a heritage building, to support screen industries; to the Briggait, a former fish market building that now contains sixty artists' studios and office space for a similar number of creative businesses. The latter also houses the Cultural Enterprise Office (CEO), which provides support to start-ups on a Scotland-wide basis. The City's infrastructure has been enhanced with a substantial virtual resource, Central Station, a social media network for the Creative Industries. Research points to these developments contributing to Glasgow being one of the most creative places in the UK. Importantly, Creative Scotland and the theme of partnership is woven through all of these initiatives.

Creative Project: Celtic Connections

Festivals are an important part of Scotland and Glasgow's creative economy as well as being a priority for Creative Scotland. They also provide a key to understanding the characteristics of the project economy. In another first Creative Scotland has collated a programme of all of Scotland's 280 annual festivals. One of the most important is Celtic Connections. Established in Glasgow in 1994 it features 1,500 artists with 300 events in 14 venues across the city, over 18 days. Apart from the cultural dimension to this international music festival it includes educational outreach and an International Showcase. The latter is important for industry development, as is the tourism impact. In 2011 there were 101,625 attendances with 25 per cent overnight stays with a direct economic impact of over £4.5 million on Glasgow and over £3.5 million on Scotland.

Quite literally, Celtic Connections networks Scotland's urban and rural music segments, especially the Gaelic world, as well as making connections to international events like Interceltique and Celtic Colours. Crucially, in terms of the rural creative economy, Celtic Connections links to Fèisean nan Gàidheal, Pròiseact Nan Ealan and the Highlands-wide Blas Festival. In fact, Celtic Connections is a good example of the creative/cultural ecology. For some this means the subsidised arts feeding the commercial arts, the voluntary arts and the amateur arts, thus ensuring creativity permeates everywhere. For others, it means the borrowing, sharing and developing of ideas. Certainly Celtic Connections has created new synergies allowing performers and musicians to come together to create new work. At the same time it has stimulated academic research. It has also spawned new commissions and created content for MG Alba, a partnership with BBC to broadcast its Gaelic TV Channel. In addition to its TV audience, through BBC iPlayer, MG Alba has notched up over 1,000,000 downloads, a substantial contributor to which, in one way or another, has been Celtic Connections.

Creative entrepreneurship and creative entrepreneurs are seen as pivotal within the Creative Economy by bridging the gap between artists and consumers (Newbiggin 2011). In that vein, creative entrepreneurship is a permeating feature of Celtic Connections with exponents like Capercaillie's Donald Shaw, Gaelic singer Julie Fowlis and Blaizin Fiddles' Aidan O'Rourke. All three variously intertwine performance, production, promotion, and cultural leadership and project management, coming together with different creatives at different times in different places to develop and deliver particular commissions or projects. What is significant is that all three prosper in the creative rural economy and use their talents and expertise to support others to do the same.

Creative Region: Highlands and Islands

The Highlands and Islands, which is both a local authority area and an economic region, covers most of Scotland geographically. A recent report on the area (HIE 2010) has indicated that its Creative Industries employ 13,285 people, in 1,670 creative businesses, generating £189m in GVA with £559m turnover per annum. Of those businesses 72% employed less than 5 people and 51% had a turnover of less than £100,000. The challenges for the area are therefore: extreme fragmentation and distance from market; problems of scale and the need to network micro-businesses; finance, especially for research and development; the supply chain and the need to understand the ecology of the area's Creative Industries.

What is striking about the Sectoral Strategy for the area is its recognition of the connective role of Gaelic, especially MG Alba and Feisean nan Gaidheal but interestingly, at the same time, the need for design-led innovation and spillovers. This has led in the latter sense to identifying priorities such as: strengthening communities; Life Sciences in terms of personalisation of product and services; Renewables, including procurement; Universities and new models and methodologies; Business services like new home-working opportunities; Tourism and its promotion; and Food and Drink linked to events, festivals and international initiatives. In turn these coalesce into strategic targets such as: growing the sector by 26% by 2017; idea development, distribution and networking; focussing on innovation skills development; integration with other sectors; festivals; and partnership with Scottish Government and Creative Scotland. Without saying so as such the Highland strategy empathises with that of rural Ontario and current European policy in the sense of seeking to promote creativity more widely both economically and socially.

Creative Place: Shetland and Orkney islands

Mareel will be the UK's most northerly creative industries centre, which is due to open in late 2011 and is a good example of Highlands and Islands' joined-up strategy. The £12 million building designed by Gareth Hoskins Architects, is situated in a prominent quayside area in Lerwick next to the new Shetland Museum and Archives. Mareel will have two cinema screens, a live performance auditorium, rehearsal rooms, a recording studio, education and training spaces, a digital media production suite and a cafe bar with free WiFi. It is a hugely important project for Shetland, culturally, educationally and economically. It will create 52 full time jobs and help with positive effects on population, especially the retention of young people. It is also intended to also raise the profile of Shetland and the Highlands and Islands internationally. UHI will deliver music and sound engineering courses and there is a multi-media production suite for film, TV, web design and digital arts. As well as providing a significant community asset in the remotest part of the UK, Mareel will also provide a supportive environment for the islands' creative entrepreneurs, particularly in terms of internationalisation and promoting creative businesses in a global marketplace.

For example, in the neighbouring island of Orkney international design company Tait and Style design and produce fabrics, which are retailed throughout Europe and Asia. Orkney is not generally thought of as one of the world's fashion centres, but it does have a tremendous pool of traditional skills, like needle punching that Tait and Style draws upon. As well as exploring the possibilities of Fair Isle and other knitting techniques, the company works with traditional knitters in the neighbouring Shetland Islands. Tait and Style has developed a reputation for innovative and unique fabrics, and for collaborations with other designers – one is Donna Wilson, a graduate of northerly Gray's School of Art, who was 2010 UK Designer of the Year. Tait and Style have also worked with Conran, Marithé and François Girbaud, Commes des Garçons, John Galliano, Dior, Shirin Guild, Givenchy, Kenzo and John Rocha.

Nurturing craft-based enterprises like Tait and Style are crucial to the remote creative economy and the company is a model of elevating indigenous human and material resources to a high level of design in which community identity is prime. Growth in Tait and Style's case is through collaboration and international networking. But remoteness and an emphasis on craft that takes its inspiration from the local environment need not be a barrier to business development and growth in terms of scale. Sheila Fleet Jewellery, also based in Orkney, employs fifty people and is expanding. The company sells through its own outlets and major department stores throughout the UK; likewise, long-established Orkney jeweller Ortak, which in 2010 turned over more than £8 million. Crafts, inseparable from design, play a crucial role in the Creative Rural Economy. Its focus on skills – on making – renders its graduates and practitioners valuable in the post-global economic crisis as the examples above seek to demonstrate. Evidence of this is provided by a study by NESTA (Bakshi 2008), which shows how art school graduates contribute to innovation both within the arts and the wider economy. The research found that these graduates possess the attitudes and skills that are conducive to innovation and that they also see themselves as brokers across disciplines. Central to the findings were experimentation and openness to new ideas, skills that are prized in the crafts, and which are valuable in the Creative Economy.

Conclusion

The Scottish Government has set a target for the Creative Economy, which is to grow by 26 per cent by 2015. Similarly, Highlands and Islands has pitched a target of 26 per cent by 2017. Key to that growth is a number of factors, not least understanding the creative ecology in which Creative Industries operate. Instrumental in that sense is encouraging research that focuses on creative entrepreneurs themselves, their experiences, activities and interactions. Intertwined with this, festivals and the project economy hold out numerous opportunities provided growth is construed in a way that is relevant to the ecology of the sector. This means appreciating growth in relation to the project economy alongside conventional business development as well as understanding the interaction between creative experience, content and service providers as identified by NESTA. Also crucial is promoting Creative Industries' spillovers into other areas of the economy. Highland and Islands identification of possible targets ranging from medical devices to social enterprise is useful in this respect. Encouraging such extreme collaboration requires a particular kind of training and development, one that is customised to the creative industries such as providing a matching-making service, design-driven innovation workshops, open innovation, industry networking and innovation camps and events.

This paper was predicated on the developmental journey of Creative Industries towards the Creative Economy and moving from an appreciation of the urban context to what it is that makes the Creative Rural Economy distinctive. It eschewed criticism of the ideological roots of the Creative Industries in favour of an incremental analysis of the evolution of the sector and its definition and redefinition to accommodate emerging economic realities. In that sense it has appeared that geography is important and it is salient that Creative Scotland's strategy also includes the contribution of place to the Creative Economy as a crosscutting objective. Creative Entrepreneurship also arose as central, linked to skills and professional development customised to the particular needs of the sector. And, it may be in this latter respect as well as encouraging overspills, that the broader Canadian categorisation of creative professions linked to Florida's identification of three sets of skills; analytical, social intelligence and physical, are worthy of consideration. Infrastructure also is absolutely essential, as is tailored support and judicious public intervention. And, of course, all of this needs strategic national coordination. Joined up creativity is the key.

32

Aberdeen Doesn't Need a 'McGuggenheim' and Shouldn't Have to Vote on it Either

Last week my 90-year-old mother-in-law received ballot papers for the City Garden Project. Like other Aberdonians she is being asked to vote on the design by New York architects Diller, Scofidio, Renfro, won in an international competition, and which the scheme's protagonists claim will have a transformational effect on the city. Like others who have lived all their lives in the Aberdeen, my mother-in-law does not like the proposed scheme but would like something to be done with the Gardens.

So, how to vote? If the American scheme is the panacea, what was the problem? It is a referendum on architecture but with no sub-structure and no touch points for the concerned citizen. That's the nub of the debacle that has convulsed Aberdeen ever since oil tycoon Sir Ian Wood offered £50 million of his own money to regenerate the sunken Victorian Gardens in the centre of the city.

Aberdeen was recently described by Jonathan Glancey, one of the UK's foremost architecture critics, as an architectural riddle wrapped in a cultural mystery inside a financial enigma. Glancey's bemusement is how Aberdeen, awash with money, has not managed to produce one building of any note in the last 25 years. It is a situation made all the more baffling by the fact that the Granite City, alongside Bath and Edinburgh, has one of the best and most readily identifiable typologies in the UK. Central to that unique architectural identity is Union Terrace Gardens. Quite how Aberdeen got into such a public tangle about a civic space, albeit a very important and central one has become an object lesson in how not to do procurement.

The problem is that every city wants a 'McGuggenheim'

believing that it will keep them ahead of the competition. Aberdeen is no exception. But the city did have a more innovative alternative. It was all the things the American scheme is not: a beautiful, cutting-edge arts centre, sensitively integrated into the site by its architects Brissac Gonzales and at a fraction of the cost. But it did not accord with the 'travelling ideas', which preferred bombast and grandiosity over elegance and simplicity.

Places which are publicly owned but which come under the control of business leaders are not democratic. Aberdeen has become a case-study in the now-universal battle between public and private. What has happened in Aberdeen not only makes a mockery of contemporary planning guidance, it undermines pledges to strengthen civic engagement and increase trust in politics. Certainly, the planning system is complex but in a well-functioning democracy it does allow ordinary people to voice what they believe the city is for and to stand up for the places they want to live in. Turning it into a yes or no vote is a travesty.

Acknowledgements

Details of the original publication of the chapters are given below.

1. Gaventa G., Ed. (1999), *The Lighthouse, Scotland's Centre for Architecture, Design and the City*, London, August Media Ltd.
2. *Visiting Rights: How Museums and Galleries Serve Their Publics*, Tate Modern, July 2000.
3. *Scotsman*, 4 August 2000.
4. *Visiting Lecture*, Duncan of Jordanstone College of Art, University of Dundee February 2001
5. *Locum Destination Review 3:2001*
6. *Representing Design 1400 to the present day*, Annual Design History Society conference, V&A, 2001.
7. Mark of the Scots, Part 4: Art & Design, *Scotsman*,11 September 2001.
8. *Scotsman* 16 January 2003
9. *Scotsman* 21 June 2003
10 *(In)visible Cities: Spaces of Risk, Spaces of Citizenship*, Centre of Contemporary Culture, (CCCB) Barcelona, 25 July 2003.
11. Star Speaker Talk, *International Architecture Biennale Rotterdam* 2003
12. macmag29 a review of the Mackintosh School of Architecture 2002-2003
13. Ford H. and Sawyers B. eds. (2003), *International Architecture Centres*, London Wiley-Academy
14. Macdonald S. ed. (2004), *Design issues in Europe Today*, Glasgow, Bureau of European Design Associations (BEDA)
15. *Sunday Herald* 11 July 2004
16. *Scotsman* 11 December 2004
17. *The Drum* 22 April 2005
18. *Scotsman* 25 June 2005
19. Lacroix M. ed. (2005*), Nouvelles Villes De Design*, Montreal, Infopresse

20. *Scotsman* 6 March 2006
21. Introduction, (2005), *6000 Miles*, Glasgow, The Lighthouse
22. *Design Week* 20 June 2006
23. MacDonald S. Ed (2006), Foreword, *Architecture in Scotland 2004-2006/Defining Place*, Glasgow, The Lighthouse
24. *Drum* 28 January 2007
25. *Scotsman* 19 May 2007
26. *Sunday Herald* 2 September 2007
27. *Crafts No 214* November 2008
28. www.scottisharchitecture.com Nov 2009.
29. *Architects Journal* 28 January 2010
30. *Neon International Digital Arts Festival*, Dundee, 2010
31. *Creative Rural Economy: From Theory To Practice Conference*, Kingston, Ontario, Canada, June 2011
32. *Scotsman* 27 February 2012

Contemporary culture has eliminated both the concept of the public and the figure of the intellectual. Former public spaces – both physical and cultural – are now either derelict or colonized by advertising. A cretinous anti-intellectualism presides, cheerled by expensively educated hacks in the pay of multinational corporations who reassure their bored readers that there is no need to rouse themselves from their interpassive stupor. The informal censorship internalized and propagated by the cultural workers of late capitalism generates a banal conformity that the propaganda chiefs of Stalinism could only ever have dreamt of imposing. Zer0 Books knows that another kind of discourse – intellectual without being academic, popular without being populist – is not only possible: it is already flourishing, in the regions beyond the striplit malls of so-called mass media and the neurotically bureaucratic halls of the academy. Zer0 is committed to the idea of publishing as a making public of the intellectual. It is convinced that in the unthinking, blandly consensual culture in which we live, critical and engaged theoretical reflection is more important than ever before.